VALUES Begin at HOME

Second Edition

Ted Ward

While this book is designed for the reader's personal enjoyment and benefit, it is also intended for group study. A Leader's Guide with Reproducible Response Sheets is available from your local bookstore or from the publisher.

VICTOR BOOKS®

A DIVISION OF SCRIPTURE PRESS PUBLICATIONS INC.
USA CANADA ENGLAND

Fifth printing, 1989

Scripture quotations are from the *Holy Bible, New International Version,* © 1973, 1978, 1984, International Bible Society. Used by permission of Zondervan Bible Publishers.

Recommended Dewey Decimal Classification: 649.7
Suggested Subject Headings: CHILDREARING, MORAL TRAINING

Library of Congress Catalog Card Number: 76-68855
ISBN: 0-89693-646-5

VICTOR BOOKS
A division of SP Publications, Inc.
Wheaton, Illinois 60187

VALUES BEGIN
AT HOME

Contents

For

Jane and Daniel

and theirs

Preface

We live in an age of high technology. What isn't so clear is that we are also living in an age of moral crisis.

Perhaps never before in the history of humankind have so many people been involved so vitally in making such difficult moral choices. These moral choices are on small matters and large. As tradition is being shaken apart throughout the world, people make all sorts of individual moral decisions that were formerly left to tradition and to habit.

We all share in moral responsibilities for and with each other, far beyond the wildest imagination of John Donne, the seventeenth-century poet who wrote, "No man is an island."

We need to gear up for the moral demands of our time. Not so long ago, some Christians had little more to talk about in the moral realm than whether going to movies was sinful. May God spare us from stumbling over the little matters while the huge issues sweep the world toward the hour of judgment. As Christians, we have to find our voices. The world is full of difficult moral issues. When will we get ourselves together?

Not until we learn how to think about and how to talk about moral values.

Moral judgment is a responsibility of all human beings. Part of growing up is the maturing of the capability to make responsible moral judgments. The development of this capability requires help from outside even though the basic process of change toward maturity is a built-in part of being human. Parents need to know something about the process and about the ways in which they can help.

In recent years many books have been written on the subject of moral development. Many of these have focused on technical issues as they relate to the scientific reader. But moral judgment and the process of moral maturity concern everyone. *Values Begin at Home* has been written with practical concerns in mind and in language that virtually any parent can understand. Only a few technical words have been used, and they are defined in the Glossary.

This book is offered as an encouragement to think more carefully about the moral issues around us and about the value choices we make day by day. It is not a book about moral propositions, as such, though I have made no special effort to conceal my own positions.

My hope is that the book will help families to talk together about moral issues and the value choices they make daily, and, beyond the talking, to find ways to act.

"You are the salt of the earth" (Matthew 5:13). Salt must be really salty if it is to have its intended effect. "You are the light of the world" (Matthew 5:14). No light is intended to be hidden. Its purpose is to enlighten and to enable people to see.

Ted Ward
Trinity Evangelical Divinity School
Deerfield, Illinois
1989

Introduction to the Second Edition

The original edition of *Values Begin at Home* was written during the flurry of excitement over Lawrence Kohlberg's research into moral reasoning. The first edition drew heavily on Kohlberg's observations but resisted the highly speculative extremes that appeared in some articles and books on moral reasoning during that period.

In the enthusiasm over Kohlberg's research, many religious educators tried to make Kohlberg's findings answer inappropriate questions. Kohlberg was not dealing with spiritual matters except indirectly. Instead, he was describing one narrow but important facet of moral judgment—the process of moral reasoning.

As they probed deeper into the meaning of his findings, some of the initial excitement waned. It seemed as if the "quick fix" was not to be found in Kohlberg after all. The very idea that a social scientist such as Professor Kohlberg would devote his research to such a matter as moral reasoning seemed to surprise many people in the field of Christian education. Further, the language that Kohlberg used to describe his findings, especially the word *justice*, seemed to have a biblical ring. What so many failed to notice was that Kohlberg's focus was very limited; he did not claim to be dealing with more than the mental processes and the social inputs to those processes. He was not treating the matter of moral behavior and was dealing only indirectly with the issue of responsible sources of moral truth. After being pushed time and again by religious educators, he began making speculative statements about these matters and thus all sorts of confusion arose. Where was Kohlberg coming from? Certainly he was not basing his speculations about moral content on either a carefully wrought Judaic theology or a Christian understanding of the Word of God.

When this lack of theological grounding became evident, many of the very educators who had teased him into answering questions that were beyond his competency turned away and began to speak and write their rejections of all of his contributions. It has become an illustration of the old habit of throwing away the baby along with the bathwater.

Since the landmark studies of Piaget and confirmation in the research of Kohlberg, the concept of developmental stages has become central within the understanding of the development of reasoning and social relationships. Thus it is common today to understand what we see in children and what we plan in education in terms of "ages and stages," referring to the rather predictable plateaus and transitions to next plateaus in the emerging competencies and dispositions of the person.

Now that many educators have turned away from two decades of ill-advised flirtation with behavioristic psychology—and the murky determinism that has resulted, there is much less influence on the field of religious education from psychological theories except within developmentalism. The developmentalists have provided a frame of reference in which the human being can be examined and understood. Their particular contributions help us to see the person, whether child or adult, as being shaped by an interaction between emerging characteristics within the person—Piaget called them psycho-genetic factors—and what goes on around the person in the environment.

Developmentalists see the social environment as being of great importance but never as the sole determinant of what the child will become. And, most important, they do not advocate a control of the environment in order to produce certain outcomes in the developing person.

This new edition of *Values Begin at Home* reaffirms my confidence in the important insights that a Christian educator and a Christian parent can gain from developmental research:

• All moral choices are reasoned choices. The materials and procedures that the human mind uses to make moral choices are of concern to parents and teachers.

• The moral reasoning process involves two facets: moral content and moral structure. When parents or teachers are concerned about only one or the other of these facets, their influence on a child's moral reasoning will be seriously limited.

• As with every other aspect of human development, the process of moral reasoning develops across time, moving from one stage or style of reasoning into another stage.

• The stages of development of moral reasoning are predictable in terms of sequence but far less so in terms of timing. Some people never develop into the higher stages of moral reasoning, and several of the probable reasons for retarded development can be identified.

• Difficulty in understanding and accepting moral messages and well-intended attempts at moral influence can be traced in many cases to the difference between the stage of moral reasoning implied in the message or the influencer and the stage of moral reasoning used by the receiver of the message.

Observations such as these are important for Christians to understand. Some of the frustrations we encounter as we attempt to help others to spiritual maturity can be traced to misunderstandings about the nature of the human being. We read in the Bible that we are "fearfully and wonderfully made," but the Scriptures are not a thorough source of data about the wonders of human development. God intended that we study His handiwork directly. Christians seem to accept this thought easily when it comes to the study of the starry heavens or the world under the microscope; but when it comes to social science—the study of the human being as person, as family, and as society, these same people tend to be suspicious and aloof. The time has come to take more seriously the study of human processes.

This book should help parents and Christian educators fulfill their unique responsibilities within the home and church. Pastors and other church professionals will find this book useful for reference and counseling. Though the book can stand alone as a valuable resource, materials are provided so that it may be used for group study.

A leader's guide provides thirteen one-hour, step-by-step plans for studying this book in a group setting. These guides may be used in adult Sunday School, Sunday evening or mid-week study series, small informal study groups, and seminars and workshops in conferences and retreats. These guides include complete study plans, learning activity instructions, visual aids, and suggestions for further investigation and reading.

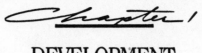

DEVELOPMENT AND VALUES

God must surely enjoy change. He created a universe that is full of change. Every living creature, the trees, flowers, rivers, lakes, seas, and even the rocks and mountains of this earth change from season to season and from year to year. Around us in the measureless space of the universe, the positions and forms of the stars and planets are constantly in process of change. Nothing stays the same except God Himself.

All living creatures change according to patterns that are part of their very nature. The human being is best understood as a creature of change. We enter this life as helpless beings "only a mother could love." The dependency of the human infant—weak, uncoordinated, incapable of any behavior that appears "intelligent"—seems an object lesson to remind us of our continuing frailty and need for help from others. God did not create other mammal forms with such lifelong dependencies and interdependencies.

Apparently, God intended that human beings move from almost helpless dependency into maturity through processes of slow and stepwise development. If we are to really understand people, we need to realize not only that each person is in a condition of change and development, but that there are certain general patterns and somewhat predictable stages in this process. The development of this remarkably dependent yet thoroughly marvelous life-form is genetically built into the human being who is at the same time interacting and being nurtured and shaped by the resources and the circumstances of the physical and social environment.

The argument still rages about the relationship between nature and nurture. It is popular to say, "Leaders are born, not made." Somehow it seems easier to believe that if two individuals' life environments are more or less similar, the differences between them must be somehow "built in" or to use the more correct word, *genetic*. Extreme examples of this view surface in the assertions that people of one race are "genetically superior" to those of another race. While there is substantial truth in the view that genetic differences (inherited factors) play a substantial part in the shaping of a person's physical and psychological characteristics, environment is also very important. In other words, the issue of *nature* and *nurture* is not an either/or matter. Both nature and nurture are important.

Parents have done their part in the genetic process by the time the child is born, but their responsibilities as parents are just beginning. Parents make immeasurable marks on the developing child through the environment they create, especially in the youngest years.

The influence of the environment is so important that some people go to yet another extreme and convince themselves that environment is everything. But to accept this view, one has to explain the often highly contrasting outcomes of childhood in brothers or sisters who have grown up together. The differences in siblings are evident in personality, motivations, tastes, and in values. There are parents who spend the rest of their lives fretting about where they went wrong with Sharon since younger sister Shannon turned out to be "such a marvelous person." It may not be that the parents treated them differently or that the sisters had different environments in which to grow. It may not even be a matter of "the crowd they hung around with." It is possible that preferences for childhood friends is traceable to a basic difference in genetic makeup.

LESSONS FOR PARENTS

Of all the lessons parents must learn, there are two that are most important. First, the development of a child is infinitely complex and cannot be completely understood or explained. On the one hand, there are certain things that can and should be understood. A major purpose of this book is to help parents learn some of these matters as they relate to moral development.

But on the other hand, there is a limit to even our best understandings. A parent can never completely explain the reasons why things happen as they do in the development of a child. "Why?" is a very difficult question to answer in reference to the differences in children. Much time can be wasted trying to turn back the pages of a family's history to correct past "mistakes" for which the parent wants to take the blame.

The second very important lesson is that the influence of parents never ceases. The moment to be grasped is *now*. It is never too late to provide the right sort of help and encouragement. It is never too late to move into a constructive relationship with the child. For sure, it may be difficult to overcome hindrances in that relationship that have come from past mistakes, but it does no good to "cry over spilled milk."

In workshops on family development and in counseling with parents, I find that mothers and fathers tend to ask many questions about details and small issues—matters that reveal their lack of a grasp of the big picture. No parents will ever find a handy guidebook to the parenting task that will give them the right answers for every question. Nor can they expect to get the most out of a learning experience such as a workshop on family development, or even reading a book such as this one, if all they are seeking is explanations for yesterday's experiences.

The more important and worthwhile goal is to gain an awareness of the larger scope of development and how a parent can work with the process rather than unintentionally undermining it. The task of parents as learners then is to discover as much as possible about how things work, what they can expect of the child's internal tendencies toward development, and how they can arrange the environment so as to support the development processes.

STAGES OF DEVELOPMENT

The evidence of stages of growth and development is substantial. The idea of stages suggests that life develops more like a stairway than an escalator. Development is not a smooth and gradual slipping upward from immaturity toward maturity; it is more like a series of flat stretches—perhaps a bit rocky, each beginning and ending with a transition that is often much more rocky. Effective parents and teachers understand children's behavior and reasoning in terms of these stages and anticipate the often turbulent transitions from one to another.

What makes development work—the "engine of development," to borrow Jean Piaget's term—is the interaction between what is going on inside and outside of the child. The pattern of changes toward maturity in every aspect of development is established within the genetic structure. The person interacting with varieties of experiences will have encounters which sometimes induce disequilibrium or being "out of balance" just enough that their system of reasoning must be reorganized. Such periods of putting things back together in new ways are the significant transitions in the development of reasoning.

In the developmental perspective, it is interaction with people that shapes lives. Thus the physical elements of an environment are less important than the people and relationships of that environment. Parents are crucial primarily because of the relationships that children can develop with them; far less important are the physical and material things and the entertaining events that money can buy.

EFFECTIVE PARENTING

Effective parenting is possible regardless of the social status and financial wealth of the family. While it certainly makes a difference if most of the parents' time and energy is necessarily spent in labor outside the home, this condition is no more hazardous for children's development than the situation that occurs among people of "substantial means" where one or both parents spend vast amounts of time and energy on career and the acquisition of more wealth and social prestige.

The quality of parenting is much more than a matter of how much time is spent in the presence of the child. One of the more recent trends is to differentiate ordinary time and *quality time* with the child. The intended emphasis concerns the extent to which the time with the child is really focused on the child and on matters he sees as meaningful and important. The assumption is that the child really needs a relatively small but regularly available experience with the father and mother—experiences which are meaningful and memorable. The contrast, of course, is the home situation in which the children are in the presence of the parents for long periods of time each day, but where nothing much passes back and forth in conversation or participating activity.

But parenting is more than a matter of "quality time."

What likely counts far more in terms of the development of the child is the willingness of the parent to engage the child where he or she really is in terms of development. While this idea is implicit within quality time, too often parents think only in their own perspective of what counts as quality. *Significant quality time is when the child is truly caught up in an experience that makes sense and communicates caring.*

One task of the parent who wants to be effective is to learn as much as possible about how the development processes work, what can be expected of the child's own internal tendencies toward development, and how the environment can be arranged so that the child's development processes are supported.

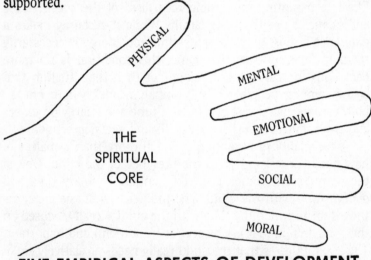

THE
SPIRITUAL
CORE

FIVE EMPIRICAL ASPECTS OF DEVELOPMENT

A HANDY PICTURE OF THE WHOLE PERSON
The development of moral reasoning is but one of the observable aspects of the developing child. We can measure and objectively describe physical development, mental develop-

ment, emotional development, social development, and moral development. Moral reasoning is closely related to spirituality, though it is surely not the same thing. Given the five empirical (observable) aspects of the development of the human being, where can we put the important matter of spiritual development?

Spiritual development is a general term for the maturing of a person's "inmost being" or the spiritual core. No one can quite put a finger on this very important center-point of what it is to be human. When God shaped the human form, He put in place many observable features that we can touch, see, hear, and measure. Moses tells us that when God breathed His own breath into this creature, Adam "became a living being" (Genesis 2:7).

Theologians for centuries have described this spiritual essence as being the center of the image of God in humankind. We must represent the spiritual nature not as merely one more of the empirical aspects—it isn't even directly observable—but rather as the special center of what it means to be a human being.

The Bible describes the person who is born again as being alive, whereas the unrepentent person who has not come to God through the redemptive work of Christ is said to be "dead in transgressions and sins" (Ephesians 2:1). We conclude then that the fact of observable liveliness in one or more of the empirical aspects is no assurance that the person is spiritually alive. These are quite different matters.

Hardly any Christian today thinks of spirituality as being separated from the rest of life. There once was a time when mysticism reigned and much emphasis was given to the rituals and abstract spiritual exercises that attempted to put all the rest of one's life in a sort of suspended animation while the center was becoming more spiritual. We should thank God that today it is more widely recognized that every part of life relates to every other part. Holism or being holistic (some write it wholistic) and other uses of this term are becoming more common. Although the word is also used by followers of Eastern meditation, it is nonetheless a valid term for the Christian view of life. Everything relates to everything else.

This principle is represented in your own hand, where you have a reminder of the way that God made you. Each of your five fingers represents one of the observable aspects of your person. But connecting it all together and giving meaning to the unity that your hand represents is the broad palm, picturing your spiritual center. Many aspects, many processes, many parts, but one whole person.

Any simple explanation of a human being is sure to be inadequate and misleading. In the Bible's descriptions, there are three or four major elements, depending on whether one assumes that soul and spirit mean the same thing: body, soul, mind, and spirit. In some texts the combination of body and *spirit* seems to embrace the whole person, as in 2 Corinthians 7:1. In other places a simple distinction is drawn between the body and the *soul,* as in Matthew 10:28. The biblical use of these categories, separately and in combination, is not consistent. Surely the Bible does not prescribe any one model of the person.

Although today's scientific awareness suggests specific aspects of the person that are not labeled in the Bible, today's views of the human being do not come down to any one precise list. There is so much overlap and interdependency that it would be foolish to argue for any one way to represent all that it means to be human.

WHAT KINDS OF
VALUES ARE THERE?

Y ou are a unique person. You are a cluster of values. That cluster is not exactly like any other. No one else is a perfect match.

Your life is shaped by the things you believe to be important. Everything you do shows your values.

What is happiness to you? What is success? What do you fear? What do you like? What is good? What is bad? What is right? What is wrong? These are *value* questions.

While this book is not about ice cream, that's where we start to look at the matter of values. Surprised? Don't be. We'll get into more important things, all in good time.

PREFERENCES OR INVESTMENTS

Some people prefer chocolate ice cream and some prefer vanilla. Maybe your favorite is strawberry or butter pecan (that's mine). Whatever you choose as your favorite flavor tells something about you. When you say, "My favorite is raspberry," or "I don't like lemon sherbet," you show something about your values. Your tastes in all sorts of things (music, art, clothes, furniture, pets) are part of what makes you the special person you are.

Values are concerned with little things as well as big. Whether you prefer chocolate or vanilla ice cream isn't really important. But how you treat other people is another matter. Your relationships express more important values than your preferences for ice cream flavors.

Preferences for flavors, colors, flowers, brand names, or styles are matters of taste. Tastes are relatively unimportant values, but they add up to a total. Can you think of a man who usually drives a Ford, dresses in blue most of the time, wears a floppy jacket, and always orders iced tea? If you know such a person, notice how easy it is to spot him by mentioning four of his tastes.

Taken one by one, your tastes are not all that important, but taken together, they add up to the *you* that others know. Very likely you wouldn't want to be known for such simple and unimportant things—you probably don't think your tastes say much about what kind of person you are—but they are part of what others see. We hope other people look deeper. But when they do, what do they see?

When Jesus talked about values, He skipped right over the matter of tastes and put His finger on investments. Where you put your money and time tells something important about you. Jesus said, "Where your treasure is, there your heart will be also" (Matthew 6:21).

Most people in North America invest in housing because they value a nice place in which to live. Whether buying or renting, an investment in housing takes a big bite out of a family's income. It also shows a value.

We buy other things. Some of these purchases we call *necessities*. Others we call *extras* or, more honestly, *luxuries*. The way we spend money shows the values that are basic in our lives.

Many North Americans are called *affluent* because they have enough money to buy things they don't need. How do we decide that we really need something? What some people call a necessity, others call a luxury. The way we make the distinction between necessities and luxuries tells something about our values. A luxury we don't have may become a necessity when we see that our neighbors have bought one. How easily we convince ourselves that we *need* things!

Time is like money. You have only so much time in a day, and you make choices about how to spend it. These choices tell much about your values.

When we think about how to use time, money, and relationships, we must look at both our deliberate choices and our habits. Some patterns of investments are based on choices and some are simply continuations of habits. We find out how important our values really are when we face an investment decision head-on and make a logical choice. But when we do things as habit, without thinking, we lose part of our self-control.

Jesus said, "Do not store up for yourselves treasures on earth, where moth and rust destroy, and where thieves break in and steal" (Matthew 6:19). These words are a warning that some of our decisions can lead to poor investments.

The good news about value decisions is that we have a built-in desire to make our own decisions. The bad news is that we have a tendency to neglect things—even important things. Neglecting to take the responsibility for good decision-making lets a lot of life fall into patterns of habit. We do things not so much because we choose to but because it's easiest to act on habit. It saves so much thinking and effort.

BASIC HUMAN NEEDS

The human infant is almost helpless. Compared with many other creatures, we arrive in this world wholly dependent. In contrast consider the African wildebeest, a large member of the antelope family. The newborn calf can stand in five minutes; in fifteen minutes it can run sufficiently well to keep up with its mother. Thus its vulnerability to predators is limited to the very short birth process itself. But human babies are born needing lots of care and warmth of affection. Because we are so helpless, we are social creatures from the start, needing to relate to other human beings.

We are born with only a few instincts—to cry out, to breathe, to turn toward warmth, to suck, to swallow. Not a very impressive bag of tricks, but it gets us through the first few months. Then, something else takes over—not more animal instincts, but behaviors we pick up from other people.

We develop a consciousness of ourselves and of what others are doing. We relate all of this in simple ways to the needs we recognize. We use our resources and we use others to meet the needs for food, light, and shelter. This is the beginning of a lifelong process of satisfying our own needs.

Abraham Maslow, a late president of the American Psychological Association, described five kinds of need that motivate human life. As the first set of needs is met, the person can deal with the second, then the third, and so on. All of these needs stay with us for life. Although they emerge more or less in the order given here, none is exclusively a childhood need.

● Physiological (bodily, physical) needs. Early in life it becomes clear that there are needs for food, sleep, and physical activity.

● Safety needs. As the child begins to move about, his safety and security are sometimes threatened. Then the need for protection from harm and injury emerges.

● Love and belongingness needs. As we develop a sense of being a person, the needs for acceptance, affection, and social approval grow. What others think becomes very important.

● Esteem needs. In adolescence and young adulthood, the

dominant needs are for self-respect, status, and proof of one's own social adequacy.

- Self-fulfillment needs. In normal adulthood, needs focus on personal growth. Matters of social skills and insights, including a sense of fulfillment, are important. The adult seeks for reassurance that life is indeed worthwhile and that he is really making a contribution to others (from *Motivation and Personality*, Harper, 1954).

How does Maslow's list of needs affect the matter of values? Take one set of needs and think about it, remembering that whatever a person finds to meet these needs will be valued.

Where do values come from? The most deeply held values come from the sense of one's needs being met. Where do the needs come from? They are part of having been created human; every human being shares in this common set of needs.

SPIRITUAL AND MORAL VALUES

What are spiritual values? Maslow's list doesn't deal with this matter, but the similarity isn't hard to see. As a person develops, he or she becomes aware that beyond the physical, social, and personal aspects there is a dimension of life that leans toward the supernatural—toward the mysteries of the universe and the purpose of life itself. The physical world asks and answers the questions of what, who, when, and where; but the *why* of life is still unanswered. A God-consciousness emerges and the person discovers spiritual need which is either met or suppressed. Whatever meets the need will be valued.

For Christians, a personal relationship with Jesus Christ is valued above all else because it meets our most basic spiritual need. Some nonbelievers meet the spiritual need through humanitarian good works. Others suppress the need through worship of the human intellect.

For the Christian, as for any religious person, spiritual

and moral values are related. One's Christian belief is surely more than fire insurance against hell. Being born again has eternal meaning, but it also has meaning for today. For one thing, the Christian is confronted with stringent demands: "I urge you, brothers, in view of God's mercy, to offer your bodies as living sacrifices, holy and pleasing to God—which is your spiritual act of worship" (Romans 12:1).

This matter of being a living sacrifice has to do with our value system. It means that our self-centered values need to be brought under God's authority. For the Christian, moral values are the vital outgrowth of religious experience. We become God's partners in a lifelong development project.

Let's look at it one step at a time. Just what are moral values? If tastes and investments are values, and ways to meet basic needs are values, what makes a value a *moral* value? Any value that affects the physical, emotional, or social well-being of even one person is a moral value.

Consider the matter of taste. Does your preference for chocolate ice cream adversely affect any human being's welfare? No, so it is not a moral issue. Try another. Is hurting someone a moral issue? Yes. Now try these questions. Is overeating a matter of moral value? Is helping an injured stranger a moral matter? What about ignoring a stranger in church?

The particular lists of "do and don't" matters in any religion fall into two clusters: the ritualistic and the moral. Among the world's religions, Christianity is rather light in the ritualistic and very heavy in the moral. Try this distinction on the following list to decide which are ritualistic values and which are moral values.

- Not stealing.
- Not being greedy.
- Being truthful.
- Respecting the rights of others.
- Bowing one's head when praying.

The first four are moral values, and the last one is a ritualistic or cultural value. Posture in prayer would no more be a moral issue or a biblical matter than whether a church building needed a steeple. Taste sometimes wanders into our values wearing a "moral" coat. Don't be taken in!

THE FAMILY AND VALUES

Through family experiences we learn many of the most important values. The family is a strong shaper of values, though it is rarely as predictable as suggested in the popular phrase, "handing down the values from generation to generation."

Today it is popular to sneer at "old-fashioned" values, even to refer to certain basic and timeless values as being "middle class." Make no mistake about it—certain values are world class, not just middle class:

● Family stability (love, respect, dependability).

● Sobriety (importance of taking certain things calmly and seriously).

● Frugality (awareness of the importance of conserving rather than wasting).

● Community responsibility (concern for one's place as a partner in a social group, in the family, in play, in public settings; cooperativeness, orderliness, and respect).

● Concern for learning (valuing the proper uses of curiosity to find out things and to enjoy new awareness and new information).

● Concern for ecology (respect for the interrelatedness of things around us—a rudimentary grasp of the way creatures depend on each other and on the environment).

These fundamental values are the sorts that the family puts in place best. By the time a child is five or six years old, values such as these are either in place within the child's awareness and habits, or they are not. And if they are not in place in a rudimentary form within these earliest years, they will be much more difficult to learn later.

Especially in light of the more common lessons learned on television—loaded as they are with violence and examples of selfish behavior and greed—today's parents have a huge task to establish an environment where children will learn alternatives to the materialism and status-climbing that seem so hard to escape in our society.

Parents need to grasp something of the developmental process as it relates to the learning of values. Understanding what is going on in the child puts a parent in a better position to be constructive. In the following chapters we will look at moral values—what they are, where they come from, how they develop, and how they connect with family relationships.

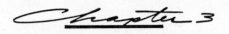

THE FAMILY
IS A VALUE

In the animal kingdom some creatures have no sense of family at all. They give birth and that's as far as the family relationship goes. But God created human beings with certain needs that call for family involvement. The human family provides shelter, protection, care, a sense of belonging, a learning environment, and a secure base from which the grown child is launched into a new family unit.

THE FAMILY

The family is especially important to Christians. God's special relationship with His people is intended to be carried out through families. In Old Testament times, parents were responsible for the spiritual and moral nurture of their children. Today's notion that schools or agencies can serve as substitute parents is not based on God's Word.

A Christian family can choose among three ways to view their duty to provide for children's spiritual and moral development. The first claims that the family is solely responsible and should not count on any outsiders to help in the moral and spiritual instruction of the children. This viewpoint is the most conservative, and in some respects it is quite biblical. It suggests the frontier family living on the edge of civilization. But this choice regards the family as a lonely island. It assumes that there are no worthwhile values in the community and little or no likelihood that any social grouping larger than the family can be developed.

The second view holds that the family is inadequate as the source of the children's moral and spiritual development. In our complex society, the family's only hope for moral and spiritual growth is in receiving outside help. At the heart of this choice is a need to transfer the family's duty to someone else. This second choice is behind the idea that churches, especially Sunday Schools, should replace the family in matters of the moral and spiritual nurture of children. More often than not, this view is not so much a conscious decision as a willingness to accept agencies, organizations, and institutions as an "easy way out."

The third view is that the family is primarily responsible. Even though help can rightly be sought, the responsibility stays in the family. This third view is a combination of the best features of the other two. It assumes that there is no way to push the responsibility for family development off onto someone else. This third view is most in harmony with Scripture.

Human development takes place over a lifetime. Close relationships with other people are important in the developmental process. It follows, then, that the family is needed to provide key learning experiences—for children and for adults.

Today's family is caught between two forces: the traditions of the self-sufficient, independent family, and the overwhelming trends toward institutionalism.

The past traditions arose as a reaction to the deplorable living conditions from which our European ancestors escaped.

In the New World, the colonists and frontiersmen pursued the ideal family environment. As the brave patriarch, the father provided for the family by his own resources. Other family members contributed effort and emotional support. Families were large enough to be small, self-sufficient communities.

Some still hold tightly to this dream and thus suffer psychological bruises when they discover that the dream is out of reach. The resulting guilt and anxiety take a terrible toll.

We must accept the fact that we are not frontier pioneers. Ours is not the "Little House on the Prairie." We live in a complex technological society. A few families can still cut wood for the fireplace, but they probably use a chainsaw produced on an assembly line. Today home-canning, weaving, and candle-making survive mostly as delightful hobbies.

THE FAMILY AND SOCIETY

Only a generation ago, one parent was at home all the time in most families. But today's cost of living often forces both parents into the working world.

Through all of this, society's institutions have taken over one by one the former duties of the family. Think about it: Whose responsibility is it to care for the elderly? Where do you go when children are born or when someone is seriously ill? Where does the money come from when you are out of work? What happens when your house burns down? There was a time when the family supplied these needs.

Today when there's a flood, the government provides substitute housing. When there's an epidemic, the public health service comes with vaccines and clinics. When there's no one at home to care for the children, the government moves in to provide day-care centers. And here's where we begin to wake up.

All of this institutionalized care is both good news and bad news. It is good news if the only alternative is suffering and neglect. But it is bad news if it encourages waste and laziness. When organized programs remove the sense of personal moral duty, they destroy important values.

In our society, neglect is everywhere, and we ease our consciences by paying more taxes. Does my neighbor have a need? Is my neighbor hungry? Thirsty? Sick? Cold? Why worry? We pay taxes to cover these needs.

But here's the problem. If our government didn't provide for these needs, people would suffer. Those who are already needy, especially people who cannot find jobs, would suffer most. On the other hand, as we use massive institutional and government programs to meet these needs, we lose the personal touch. We become less human and more mechanical. What can be done? No one seems to know.

The family unit is one of the serious casualties in this process of dehumanization. *Newsweek* reported a variety of troubling observations. Since the survey was made, the situation has become even worse.

Parents feel increasingly powerless in the face of institutional interference. The growth of social services, health care and public education has robbed them of their traditional roles as job trainers, teachers, nurses, and nurturers. And their control over their children's lives is threatened by the pervasive—and increasingly authoritative—influences of television, school and peer groups. "Our oldest daughter is only 7, and already we can see the peer pressure at work. . . . She'll come home and tell us that so-and-so has this and why don't we? . . . I know she needs social exposure, but at the same time we'd like to shelter her from other people's values—like television, easy money, and the idea that you have to go here and go there to have fun."

In their confusion, parents have increasingly turned

to experts for advice—and in the process ended up relinquishing more responsibility. . . . "By convincing the housewife and finally even her husband to rely on outside technology and the advice of outside experts, the apparatus of mass education—the successor to the church in our secularized society—has undermined the family's capacity to provide for itself," says University of Rochester historian Christopher Lasch (Kenneth L. Woodward, et al, *Newsweek*, 5/15/78) pp. 64–65, 67.

The secular society has gradually accepted the default of the family. Already a search has begun to find something to replace it. A growing number of children in the United States are raised in single-parent households. The estimate is now one out of seven. Welfare systems and public institutions are expected to care for health, nutrition, protection, and basic learning needs that formerly were a family matter. With a little imagination, we can easily picture public agencies that will be responsible for the child's moral development as well.

THE CHRISTIAN FAMILY

The traditional family is dying of neglect and disinterest. Aside from certain unpopular voices among religious and certain secular leaders, few mourn the passing of the stable family.

Today well over half of all mothers of school-age children work outside the home. Paul Glick, senior demographer for the U.S. Bureau of the Census, says that four families in ten are now becoming reconstituted families after divorce and remarriage before the youngest child reaches the age of eighteen. Beyond this statistic are the hundreds of thousands of children who are reared by only one parent.

These facts bring us to those crucial values that should distinguish the Christian family. Regardless of the particular style or structure of the family, three basics exist: *love, fidelity* (between marriage partners), and *responsibility* (especially for the loving nurture of the children).

Fidelity is at stake today. All of us are victims, to some degree, of today's loose sexual standards. The Bible persistently warns against taking sexual matters lightly. Why such emphasis on sexual standards in the Bible? Because the sexual relationship is part of the family foundation.

Responsibility is also at stake. The depersonalized society makes it easy to shirk any sense of duty. Indeed, some words are becoming meaningless—*responsibility, duty, obligation.*

The home where Christian love, fidelity, and responsibility are taught is honoring to God. With this kind of background, biblical concepts are easier to understand. The Bible uses the imagery of *father* to describe God and *family* terms (sonship, brothers, sisters, birth, adoption) to explain relationships among Christians. How can you understand these ideas if you have never experienced them? With no point of reference, these descriptions become abstract concepts.

Many people have never had a warm, loving relationship with their fathers. With such deprived backgrounds, no wonder so many fail to understand the biblical description of God as a loving Father.

The basic principles of the family, like all moral principles, are universal. They are God-given through the creation and are reaffirmed generation after generation from within the nature of humankind. If we believe in basic moral principles, we must also realize the importance of cultural differences. Any particular principle can be fulfilled in various ways, depending on the culture. For example, *family* is a value; the basic principles upon which family is built are *fidelity* and *responsibility* as fulfillments of *love.*

Does this argue for a *nuclear* family (mother, father, and children) as it has been historically in North America? Or does it rather support the idea of an *extended* family (all the aunts, uncles, and grandparents too) so typical in parts of Europe, Asia, and Latin America? Does it suggest that *tribal* families (where cousins by the dozens all think of each other as brothers and sisters) are somehow unbiblical? No, to all of these questions.

We should respect the different ways important principles are fulfilled. We should not have major arguments over anything less than the basic principles. In matters of family, let's concentrate on the moral principles of love, fidelity, and responsibility. Through these, the family *is* a value.

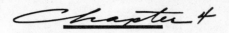

WHERE DO GOOD VALUES COME FROM?

This book is for Christians. Anyone who loves the Lord Jesus Christ also loves God's Word and values God's Law. The Christian has a unique way of approaching matters of values. The Christian determines what is right or wrong differently than does the person who does not know God through Jesus Christ. Even when the Christian and the morally motivated non-Christian come to the same conclusion on a matter of good and evil, the Christian has likely taken into account some factors that do not have a place in the other person's reasoning.

Religious people, in general, are criticized for being too sure of themselves. Maybe it is a fair criticism. Surely someone whose feet are on a rock will slip less than someone whose feet are in mud. With the conviction that Christ is the answer, we are putting our confidence in a sure foundation.

However, people who seem to have all the answers are frequently resented. In some ways we Christians often appear "to have it all together" and thus to lack patience with others—even our own kids. In Christ, we have found the way, the solid foundation, the truth, the real life. It's easy to stop right there, feet on the rock, head in the clouds, and crow about it. What bystander wouldn't be at least slightly turned off?

Just let a Christian gain some spiritual maturity and the bystander will sing a different tune. At first, the complaint was that the Christian was shallow and trite. Now the onlooker sees a level of spirituality emerging and begins to criticize the Christian's tendency to be aloof and too isolated from the "real world." But when the Christian's spiritual depth develops into a deep burden for God's work of redeeming the world, the critic complains that no one has any right to be so confident.

Consider Jesus and His onlookers. Jesus said, "I am the way and the truth and the life. No one comes to the Father except through Me" (John 14:6). Was this any way to make a hit with the crowd? Hardly. But Jesus said it because it was true. Like it or not, the crowd couldn't possibly make sense out of what Jesus said and did unless they faced up to this basic fact.

OVERLAPPING VALUES

What Christians value based on God's Word overlaps with what morally upright nonbelievers value because of traditional social ethics. In several specific matters, the heritage of North Americans has been strongly influenced by Christian values. For example, the valuing of an orderly society based on laws that respect and defend the rights of individuals, as well as of society as a whole, is quite evidently based upon a straight historical line of biblical influence.

But there are important differences. The Christian does not see orderliness and justice as independent values which human beings are free to discover or not discover. The issue is not whether society is wise enough to think up these great values but whether people are wise enough to accept God's values.

The important question is, "Who says so?" Mankind, apart from God, tends to rely on wisdom from within. Thus, in the years ahead, as modern man attempts more and more to prove that God is unnecessary, we can expect increasing clashes over important issues of right and wrong. The easy acceptance of abortion is just the latest example. What will be next?

Rebellion began in the Garden of Eden with "Did God really say . . . ?" The first words of the serpent ask, in effect, "On whose authority have you decided how you should act? Who says so?" It is a very natural question for an unbeliever. Anyone who believes that there is no God, or that we cannot know what God is or what God values, assumes that anything which has been said or written must have a human source. Behind everything is a person or group of persons. So it is always a fair question to ask, "Who says so?" and whenever one doesn't like what has been said, to bring it back to a matter of personal argument: "Who is he to say? What special right or superior knowledge does she claim to have?"

The secular humanist comes to many of the same conclusions about good and evil as the Christian. Therefore he is likely to challenge the Christian's source. Knowing his own sources to be human philosophy, personal moral sensitivity, and educated insight, the humanist doesn't see why the Christian would want any different sources. What sort of pompous bigotry would cause a person to claim to have heard from a particular god?

Thus it always will be. How sad that secular humanity, even in its most highly moral decisions and behaviors, denies the power and the authority that lies behind all goodness (2 Timothy 3:5). Those who do not know God argue for other ways to explain everything. To them, the earth and skies are a reality, not because of God's creative work, but as the fallout of some cosmic accident. Humankind is the biological marvel of the universe, not because of God's special act of creating us "in His own image," but because of random spontaneous changes, natural selection, and evolution.

Human creations in art, science, and technology do not reflect God's creative nature showing forth in humankind but result solely from genetic factors and education. A person's persistent coping with moral matters of truth, justice, and mercy does not mean that God imparts these concerns. Instead, the humanist believes that we cope with these moral issues because we aspire to goodness through our intellect, our awareness of history, and the evolution of philosophy.

One result of this spiritual blindness is a tendency to scoff at virtue. In every age the forces of evil make humanists their unwilling accomplices. Of any statement of the basic difference between good and evil, the humanist asks, "Who says so?" The more blatant voices of cynicism make this question of doubt the cutting edge of their sword. People cannot provide their own source of release from the continuous struggle between the values of God and the values of evil. God provides the way, but His statements are challenged and often disregarded. Thus, apart from knowing Jesus Christ, people—no matter how brilliant—are lost.

KNOWLEDGE OF THE TRUTH

In our time, especially with the scientific discoveries about the nature of moral judgment, it is becoming less popular to hold to any statements of moral principles. Today, the emphasis is on moral process; educational programs that use "values clarification" simply do not go far enough. They are useful in that they focus the value issues and problems that otherwise tend to get ignored in school; but many such programs shy away from the reality that there are, indeed, matters of right and wrong. When the question of moral *truth* is raised, we find how thoroughly the humanists are in command.

Make no mistake about it: the Christian is concerned with

moral judgment both as *process* and *content*. It is very important that we see that the Word of God provides moral content. We do not need to search to discover what is good and beautiful. God puts it right on the line. His platform of moral content is specific. In the Bible, three kinds of material help us see the moral foundation:

● God's laws, especially in the Old Testament's statements of God's commandments;

● moral examples and object lessons, seen in the experiences of people and their dealings with God;

● the life and teachings of Jesus Christ and His first followers.

Yes, God provides a platform or foundation; things are not so wishy-washy as many people would have us believe. But, beyond this, God expects people to reason things out. He expects us to make choices and decisions, to use the moral judgment that is a key feature of being human.

Once when some people were trying to trap Jesus on a political issue, they asked Him if He thought it right that Jews should pay taxes. The issue was that such taxes were being collected by the occupying Roman government, which was not exactly on the best of terms with the Jewish people. Jesus asked to see the particular coin in which the taxes were to be paid. "Whose picture and name are on this coin?" He asked. "Caesar's," came back the answer. "Well, since Caesar has his marks all over it, it must belong to him. Give Caesar what belongs to him, and give to God what belongs to God." (See Matthew 22:15-22.)

This sounds simple at first, until it dawns on you. He put the responsibility for judgment right back on the people. Jesus expects mature people who hear the principle to act on it.

"Finally, brothers, whatever is true, whatever is noble, whatever is right, whatever is pure, whatever is lovely, whatever is admirable—if anything is excellent or praiseworthy—

think about such things" (Philippians 4:8).

Take a close look at these qualities: true, noble, right (just), pure, lovely, admirable—what a list! You may say, "All sweetness and light; big, fat, useless generalizations." Or you can get serious about it and say, "God is asking me to look closely and to judge." Is it truthful? Is it right and pure? If not, God is not honored.

Is my life honorable, respectable, and respectful? If not, God won't be pleased. Is it just? God invites each of us to join in the quest for justice; is there anything more exciting?

The human condition veers away from justice until all sorts of injustice hold sway, even in the nation that we most love. The good news of Jesus Christ is threefold: to those imprisoned in their own sins, to those who suffer in a handicapped condition, and to those who are victims of human injustice (Luke 4:18-21). We do not honor God if we fall short on these matters, including the responsibility to act on behalf of those who are discriminated against.

Are my actions pure? God's own purity is the measuring stick; how rarely will we find something to be pure—but it is nonetheless our concern. Is my life lovely? Not lovely in the superficial sense, but with the meaning of being crafted with loving hands. God is worthy of our best for His glory.

Those who take the Bible seriously see the importance of these qualities. They are part of the teachings of our Lord and of the apostles and they relate to our lives. For the Christian, strength of character is shaped and determined by the response we make to these teachings. Do we really want to be Christlike?

FRUIT OF THE SPIRIT

The works of God in a person's life are sometimes called the "fruit of the Spirit." These effects provide an interesting list: "But the fruit of the Spirit is love, joy, peace, patience, kindness, goodness, faithfulness, gentleness, and self-control. Against such things there is no law" (Galatians 5:22-23).

Is there any need to grope around wondering what it means to develop in godliness, as holy saints in the process of redemption? The letters to the Galatians (5–6) and to the Ephesians (4–5) are gold mines for study of the key values of Christian life. Here are a few of the nuggets of gold:

● "Carry each other's burdens, and in this way you will fulfill the law of Christ" (Galatians 6:2). Note that the "law of Christ" refers to the new commandment that Jesus gave His followers: "Love one another. As I have loved you, so you must love one another" (John 13:34). Loving as Jesus loved is not a selfish love; it is a giving, other-centered, burden-bearing love. This quality is a key value for the Christian.

● "Let us not become conceited, provoking and envying each other" (Galatians 5:26). The Christlike life makes little room for self-congratulation and seeking after honors. Cutting others down, envying, pride, competing in order to advance oneself at the cost of others—these are things to avoid.

● "I urge you to live a life worthy of the calling you have received. Be completely humble and gentle; be patient, bearing with one another in love. Make every effort to keep the unity of the Spirit through the bond of peace" (Ephesians 4:1-3). Patience—how demanding a virtue! Patience that gives the road to others. Patience that builds unity and strives for peace. But many of us are selfish. Because of our selfishness, God keeps reminding us that He honors patience—the kind of patience that only He can develop.

● "Get rid of all bitterness, rage and anger, brawling and slander, along with every form of malice. Be kind and compassionate to one another, forgiving each other, just as in Christ God forgave you" (Ephesians 4:31-32).

Nothing is more important in showing Christlike love than a willingness to forgive and the humility to ask for and accept forgiveness. Being a Christian puts a person in the middle of a continuous forgiving situation; since none of us is perfect, God continues to forgive as we confess our sins. In turn, we welcome the occasions in which by forgiving we restore relationships with our family and friends. Indeed, forgiveness too is a key value.

All of these values we call *good* because God does. They are to form the basis of our judgment. God is willing to forgive when our behavior falls short. God has created us so that our judgment, as surely a everything else about us, has to develop. Our behavior at any stage of life is based on whatever our judgment has become to that point. But since we rarely behave up to the best of our judgment, our behavior often needs to be forgiven.

As we look further into the matter of moral judgment, bear in mind that God is concerned about more than how well we reason. God is concerned about our moral *action*. And in His Word, moral action is clearly defined. The values of Christianity add up to one thing—a person—Jesus Christ, our Lord. Through Jesus Christ we see moral action; through Him we also find forgiveness.

Chapter 5

GOD'S LAW
AND CHRISTIAN VALUES

Rules and laws are not popular today. Many people resent the idea that there are certain things they *must* do and other things they *must not* do. I recall from childhood how often we answered, "Who says so?" "Yeah, you and who else?" "Well, I won't do it because I don't want to." Today not only children talk this way; adults who "do their own thing" are quick to react against rules and regulations. The whole world seems beyond reach of authority, unless the authority uses force—or unless people happen to agree with the rules.

Those who "take laws into their own hands" and those who call attention to inequity and injustice by engaging in nonviolent civil disobedience range from the self-centered to the highly principled. However, they share one thing in common—they are challenging the existing social system. On the one end of this array of people are those who seek only to gratify themselves; on the other end are those such as Bishop Tutu, Mahatma Gandhi, and Martin Luther King, Jr., who accept the consequences of their disobedience to what they see as unjust laws; they act in the spirit of calling society to engage more surely in the quest for justice.

In recent years, the whole world seems more aware of the danger in blindly following after law and order. We have seen innocent people hurt in the name of law and order. The people who talk the loudest about law and order often turn out to be vicious and lawless. We have even seen moral people picking which laws to obey in terms of personal preferences.

For example, what does it mean when a "Jesus Saves" bumper sticker goes down the highway at 79 miles per hour? What does it mean when a person who has complained about unfairness treats others unfairly? What does it mean when armies and police occupy and control the lands or properties of other people in the claim of liberating them? Such questions are all around us. It really isn't a very fair world. No wonder that people have learned to be suspicious of law and order.

Unfortunately, these suspicions spill over on God's laws. Is this new? Perhaps it is a deeper tendency than it was a generation ago. But historically, we can see the inclination to overlook or choose against God's way ever since the Garden of Eden.

When Christians refer to God's Law, they usually mean the Ten Commandments or Decalogue. When God gave the Law to Moses on Mount Sinai and carved the commandments in stone, it was not the first time that God's people heard about His moral standards. Many years earlier, Joseph had known that adultery was wrong. Moses had known that it was wrong to kill the Egyptian soldier. When the law was written down on the tablets of stone, the only thing new was the written record.

God created us and He intended that we should share with Him the awareness of moral responsibility. Because of the way God made us, His Law is embedded in our consciences. In the letter to the Romans, the Apostle Paul said that even those who have never heard of the written law have *within them* the awareness of God's Law (Romans 1:18-20; 2:14-15).

Every nation and tribe finds some way to deal with murder, theft, unfaithfulness, and also with their awareness that there is a deity to be worshiped. Such moral responsiveness is a part of being human. To clarify these matters and to find the universal standard, Christians turn to God's written Word. Because we can read what God has said, we know what lies at the heart of right and wrong.

Does this clarity help us or hinder us? Because we have before us God's Law, are we less free? Would we be better off if we had no basis of moral order?

GOD'S LAW

God's Law can be seen in two different ways. Those who resent rules see God's Law as a nuisance, or worse, they see it as the reason for their problems—"Why can't God leave us alone?" Those who know of God's love see God's Law as a generous act of kindness. If God hadn't cared about us, why would He have bothered to point out the basic moral rules of life?

God in His love has given us His moral map to help us in the confusing, shifting, slippery twists and turns of life. We can be confident in God's Word. Thus we don't have to try everything to find the harm in it, nor do we have to waste ourselves in moral blindness wondering where we went wrong.

Since there are moral dangers, it is important to know about them. It is sad when people are so independent that they resent being warned of a slippery spot in the trail or a scorpion in a sleeping bag. Those who seem determined to hurt themselves take offense at God's Law, seeing it as a set of restrictions.

Restrictions? Take a good look at the Ten Commandments and you discover that the direction of the statements is positive. Even those commandments that say "don't" are really very liberating; they suggest some good thing to *do*. They are worded as *don't* statements because they are very important warnings about behavior.

Christians should think specifically about the personal nature of each of the Commandments. While our salvation does not depend on keeping these Ten, keeping God's Law is a mark of God's people. Our happiness and the quality of life itself will be affected by how we use these statements to bring order into our lives. Considering the dozens of matters that God could have talked about as laws, it is significant that He narrowed them down to ten. They must *really* be important.

I. "I am the Lord your God . . . you shall have no other gods before Me" (Deuteronomy 5:6-7). Everyone worships something. Sooner or later the god of your life becomes obvious to those around you, even if you are not aware of it. To put the Lord God, Creator of the universe, first in your life is a marvelous place to start. From this commitment, all other values find their proper place.

For some of us, our natural self-centeredness becomes a god and we worship a mirror. For others, the appetites of greed become a god. These gods enslave; they cannot liberate. The pagan and "new age" gods of superstitious religion and witchcraft trap people in fear or in false confidence. The gods of selfish wealth and pleasure will enslave drug users, those who seek material and social success over all other values, and those who boldly make their own rules in matters of sexual behavior, just as surely as they will enslave all others who do not put God in first place.

We can be grateful that God lets us see that the first rule for an orderly life is to give Him preeminence. By doing so, we discover that being a servant of the Most High God is a liberating relationship. It liberates us from the false gods that otherwise would make us their slaves.

II. "You shall not make for yourself an idol. . . . You shall not bow down to them or worship them; for I, the Lord your God, am a jealous God, punishing the children for the sin of the fathers . . . but showing love to thousands who love Me and keep My commandments" (5:8-10). The second commandment is a clear warning against idolatry. God warns us that nothing should come between us and Himself. In our culture, idolatry is not a matter of little shrines with stone gods on shelves, but we do have trouble with symbols.

We look around for symbols or emblems to represent our experiences. Consider the apparently harmless matter of collecting stickers from each place you visit on a trip. The valuable experience, the *reality*, is the trip. The sticker or decal is but a symbol to which you attach your memories. So what's the problem? Sooner or later the matter of searching for and buying the stickers becomes the major reason for travel. I have seen people making themselves miserable wasting valuable time looking for those status-symbol stickers. How easily our graven images become outward shows that hinder the *real* experience.

God intends us to be free from the tendency to let symbols replace reality. He is our Lord in *fact*, not in fantasy. Notice how this commandment ends with a focus on love. God wants us to show steadfast love. The reality is the relationship. Wearing a cross to symbolize a relationship with Christ is surely no sin, but God warns that symbols can crowd out the reality.

III. "You shall not misuse the name of the Lord your God" (5:11). Here is a commandment that people like to complain about. Because it's a *don't* statement, you have to think twice to see what might be liberating about it. Notice that it doesn't refer to those less creative forms of swearing that arise from preoccupation with basic biological functions. The commandment refers to God's name and is concerned with a sense of respect and reverence. To be so aware of God's presence that you wouldn't want to be disrespectful is liberating.

Using God's name—or anyone's name—in vain involves an offense to the person. Swearing is evil because it attacks the dignity and honor to which God—or a person created in God's image—is entitled.

You know what happens to your relationship with a friend or family member if you get so careless that you offend that person without even meaning to. How can you be free from harming the relationship? By staying on such close terms that nothing offensive comes between you. This is what God wants. Stay close and you won't be careless about His reality or His name.

IV. "Observe the Sabbath Day by keeping it holy. . . . Six days you shall labor and do all your work. . . . Remember that you were slaves in Egypt and that the Lord your God brought you out of there with a mighty hand and an outstretched arm. Therefore the Lord your God has commanded you to observe the Sabbath Day" (5:12-15).

More silliness has been loaded onto this commandment than any other. Since the earliest years of the church, the day of special meeting and religious observance for Christians has been the *first* day of the week. Sabbath means seventh, but there is no need to change this commandment. Christians hold to the seventh, but put the emphasis on the *first* seventh, not the last seventh.

With the exception of a few groups, Christians don't keep the Sabbath. Do we stand before God unrighteous because of this failure to "keep Sabbath"? As Jesus pointed out to the Pharisees, lots of issues are more important: "The Sabbath was made for man, not man for the Sabbath" (Mark 2:27). This means that the Sabbath was a symbol of liberation in itself. How sad that we have let the Sabbath matter become an oppressive burden. The basic principle of the Sabbath deals with respect for the completeness of creation. The finished work of Christ at Calvary also has to do with completeness, but of the *new* creation.

Why was the Sabbath established? Take a good look at the text from Deuteronomy. The word *therefore* in the text is a clue that the *why* has just been stated: once you were slaves in Egypt, but now you are free!

So the Sabbath does *not* represent Israel being humbled into a day of inactivity by God, but it was just the opposite. For a people who had been forced to work day in, day out, as slaves, the Sabbath was a great shout of praise that they no longer had to work for others and for an ungodly kingdom, but for themselves and for the kingdom of God. The Sabbath is a great day of happiness, smiles, and family, focused on liberation. God has liberated us from drudgery and from being required to serve the secular system.

Is it different for Christians? It shouldn't be. Yes, we celebrate the first day, Sunday, the first one-seventh of the week. We celebrate liberation at the beginning of the week—deliverance *into* a new life in Christ. Our slavery in sin is equivalent to the Jewish experience in Egypt. God has led us into His promised land, the kingdom of God. But the parallel ends here.

The new deliverance is not through Moses, but through Christ who sits at the right hand of God the Father. Our salvation is in the shed blood of Jesus Christ, Son of God, Redeemer, who was raised from the dead on the first day of the week. Our Sabbath is not only for God's week of work in creation; even more our celebration is for deliverance *into* the "new week" of life in Christ. The early Christians, with their rapidly developing insights into the principles of the Old Testament, spotted all of this symbolism and shifted their Sabbath Day observance into the first day of the week, the day of new beginnings. The Lord's Day!

The most satisfying and God-honoring way to observe the principle of the Sabbath is to set apart one-seventh of the week as a personal, family, and church observance of the celebration of deliverance and liberation. God makes us free. On the first day of the week, we are reminded through special gatherings of the church for worship that there is more to life than the pressures, the demands, and the drudgery of the normal routine. Show me a Christian who treats the Lord's Day like any other, and I'll show you a tired and frustrated Christian.

V. "Honor your father and your mother" (5:16). The importance of home and family within the Christian community is underlined in this commandment. It is within the family that the child first realizes that he is a moral decision-maker. The moral environment of the family, particularly the value choices of the parents, is of great importance to the child's development.

Since every human must take those first steps of discovery to find right and wrong, the relationship with parents is crucial. If parents are doing as God intended, they are providing consistent clues about what is right and what is wrong. The child reaches out, explores, and receives the clues that are needed. Those clues must be reliable.

The earliest awareness of moral conscience is simple: some things are right and some things are wrong. The child's moral sense is thus developed. It is important that the child's relationship with the major source of those clues, the parents, be filled with respect and love.

Is this commandment more concerned with what children ought to do or what parents ought *to be?* God's commandment is *to honor* father and mother. The emphasis here is not obedience (though it is included), but respect. Anyone with power can make others obey. But only an honorable person can expect to be honored.

VI. "You shall not murder" (5:17). Only four words, but

they are important. When Jesus wanted to explain the difference between law and principle, He started with something everyone could understand: this law (Matthew 5:21).

Even people who resent God's list of "don'ts" seem happy enough about this command. Life itself is violated by killing. No society can endure unless it deals with killing.

The terrorists of our time show that the government which cannot deal with killing is no government at all. This is evident in the random bombings, senseless shootings, and political kidnappings. Killing is the most powerful form of evil communication.

But is killing ever justified? God told Israel to clear the land of evil through warfare. God authorized executions for certain crimes. Yet God did not use the death penalty on murderers such as Moses and David.

I can turn my other cheek to *my* enemies, as God gives me strength. But can I watch you be tortured and killed without defending you? It's not easy to say. Even God's Law doesn't reduce life to a series of black and white push buttons. We are moral creatures. We must observe. We must participate. We must deal wisely with difficult questions.

Where do we stand on the issue of war? What would make a vast shedding of blood a "just" war? What is the moral alternative to war? What is the morality of conscientious objection to war? Historically, Christians have led the Western world in dealing with these issues. We must continue to lead; our God has been explicit about murder. Where does this put us regarding the complicated variations on the theme of killing? While we are at it, we should ask again just how early in life a person can be killed without calling it murder.

VII. "You shall not commit adultery" (5:18). This commandment always seems to get too much or too little attention. People either know so little about it that it seems unimportant to discuss, or they know so much about it that they are afraid to discuss it. Either way, the matter of adultery is not a popular discussion topic.

As a matter of fact, this Law is not nearly so related to sex as it is to the matter of faithfulness and interpersonal integrity. When the Old Testament prophets used illustrations based on adultery, they were always dealing with the relationship of God's people to God Himself.

In biblical terms, adultery violates the most basic and essential human relationship—the relationship of husband and wife. God isn't trying to keep us from having fun or to trap us with restrictions. Instead, He is warning us that no truly liberated life can be built apart from a sense of moral faithfulness.

The old-fashioned notion of a husband and wife being faithful to each other is still the key to happiness and stability in the home. Even the secular society seems to be getting fed up with its own carelessness in matters of sex and marriage. Perhaps the new and frightening awareness of AIDS has brought many people to their senses; but even as marriage was ripped open by the pill and hedonistic selfishness, it may be possible to heal the wounds with a combination of awareness that sin's price is high and a gracious outworking of the spirit of reconciliation through those who are faithful to Christ and to their marriage vows. In any case, Christians know that sexual faithfulness is basic; without faithfulness, the endless rounds of suspicions, uncertainties, and sneakiness create such emotional bondage that there is no sense of freedom.

Sexual desires are a fact of life, and Christians are no different from the rest of the human race. We happily acknowledge our sexuality, because God has made us. The sexual experience is the human celebration of love, the ultimate in giving and receiving, the physical renewal of oneness in body and spirit, and the symbol of God's involvement with human beings. But most importantly, it is the emotional bond that holds the husband and wife together as the ups and downs of life bash against the door.

Is sexual experience a value for a Christian? Yes. Sex in its right place is vitally important and a powerful positive value for a Christian. However, outside of marriage it is a negative value—and not because we are against the experience itself. Rather, it is because we are so much for it that we don't want to see it damaged. God's Law points toward liberation. How can a person be truly free while being victimized by the compulsions of his or her animal instincts?

VIII. "You shall not steal" (5:19). One of the earlier experiences of childhood is a sense of ownership: *my* mother, *my* toy, *my* food, *my* bed. Let any of these be "stolen" and the reaction is quick.

As children grow up, this sense of ownership expands and matures. Some children learn that things they find at school which belong to others should be returned and that they are responsible for their own work and should not cheat themselves by copying from others.

But because of sin in the human heart, it is "natural" to covet and even to steal. The wider consequences of a misplaced value of ownership can lead to serious social consequences, including encounters with the harsher forms of law enforcement systems.

For many young people, stealing begins with an exaggeration of the importance of ownership. Property and possessions become a consuming obsession. "That car, boat, television, stereo is mine. I bought it; I made it; I earned it; it was given to me. What's mine is mine."

It isn't quite so easy to say, "What's yours is yours." A thread of "grab it" is woven into human nature. Even when we know better, a tendency to reach out and take what isn't ours sometimes slips in.

Every society deals somehow with stealing, but they may not all define it the same way. For example, in parts of Latin

America anything left unattended, even a bicycle left outdoors at night, is assumed to mean, "I no longer want this. If you need it, help yourself." But a person might be treated to a slashing knife if the bicycle were taken from the *inside* of the house.

Indeed, orderliness in a family and in a nation depends on a clear idea of what is and what isn't right in matters of property. Is it wrong to exploit others by accepting things that are theirs before they are aware of their value? Is it stealing to give a person four quarters for a dollar bill? Hardly. But what if you make the trade knowing that the dollar bill is a collector's item? Christians must face these issues because God's Word teaches that stealing is wrong.

IX. "You shall not give false testimony against your neighbor" (5:20). The ninth commandment deals with truth. As God's children, we are to be people of truth. Truth is a basic value in the Christian community. Lying and slander are OUT. We should even think twice about the little white lies that make things "nice"—half-truths, exaggerations, and insincere compliments. Our commitment to truth should be as complete as the limitations of being mortal will allow. We regard trustworthiness as one of the marks of God being in us. Flattery or deceptive praise for manipulative and self-seeking purposes is dishonest; but that should not keep a well-behaved person from being kind and positive in relationships to others.

Christians do not uphold truth by saying things that are only technically correct. Bearing false witness suggests that one is telling something untrue about another. But it also covers two other kinds of untruthfulness.

What about silent withholding of the truth? If a judge asks, "Did anyone see this man on the night of August 12?" and you did and don't speak up, you may not have told a lie, but you have been a false witness. For the Christian, a statement is untruthful if it is misleading. The issue is more than the lie; it is false testimony.

What would happen if we were constantly deceiving each other? If you couldn't count on what anybody said and you knew nobody believed you either, would you feel very free? Of course not. Is God's Law a burden? No, once again it points to the liberation that comes from orderliness.

X. "You shall not covet your neighbor's wife. You shall not set your desire on your neighbor's house or land, his manservant or maidservant, his ox or donkey, or anything that belongs to your neighbor" (5:21). God's Law separates covetousness (desiring what doesn't belong to me) from stealing. Here the emphasis is on that "innocent" backyard sport of wishing I had my neighbor's boat. I'd never think of stealing it, but what's the harm in dreaming about it? In Colossians 3:5, the Apostle Paul put coveting together with greediness and called it all idolatry. The Ten Commandments end with a reminder that when *things* become our god, our relationship with God is damaged. Then other relationships begin to suffer.

Jesus urged His followers to guard themselves against covetousness—He called it an uncontrolled desire for wealth and a greedy longing to have more. A man's life does not consist in the abundance of his possessions (Luke 12:15). On this subject Jesus told the parable of the farmer who became so rich that he tore down his storage bins to build larger and larger. Suddenly he was dead. Who would all this grain belong to now? Such a greedy farmer is a person "who stores up things for himself, but is not rich toward God" (Luke 12:21).

One of the major goals of commercial television is to convince people to buy things. Thus everyone who watches even a few hours a week is being stimulated to covet. While this commercialism is within the bounds of legal marketing, it is nevertheless foolish to expose ourselves and our children to such steady inducement to grasp for more and more material things. Eventually human beings could become like sharks at feeding time—frenzied. (Have you heard of the wife of the former President of the Philippines?)

God warns about the road to enslavement in materialism. Choose instead the liberation of God-centered and people-focused humanity. The Law of God is aimed at building and keeping the integrity of people.

THE VALUE OF THE LAW

The Apostle Paul was educated in a legalistic tradition. Before becoming a Christian he was a highly respected Pharisee. As a Christian, he knew that God's Law was valuable and good. Yet he saw how useless it was to build a road to God based on keeping the Law.

Paul's answer to the matter of Law has two elements. First, a person can stand before God's judgment either as a proud keeper of the Law or as a humble sinner claiming God's grace. If one attempts to stand in self-righteous pride, all the little flaws will show, no matter how good the behavior. The other way to stand, in humility claiming only Christ's righteousness, offers the only possibility of experiencing God's grace. Every person who comes to God through the blood of Jesus Christ knows the truth of Paul's affirmation: "He saved us, not because of righteous things we had done, but because of His mercy. He saved us through the washing of rebirth and renewal by the Holy Spirit, whom He poured out on us generously through Jesus Christ our Saviour" (Titus 3:5-6).

What, then, is the value of the Law? Paul said that the Law is like a teacher or guide (Galatians 3:24-25). It teaches us that God is a moral God who is very concerned about matters of good and evil. We must make moral decisions in life. Through the Law, God gives us a solid foundation that makes it possible for us to deal with life's moral choices.

To cover all the issues and decisions about right and wrong would require thousands of laws. The Pharisees had made a good start on creating such a list. They had a law for everything they could think of. They stubbornly insisted that everything in life be viewed as a matter of law. It is no wonder that the Pharisees were so displeased with Jesus. He said that He came to fulfill the Law, yet it was obvious that He didn't approve of the Pharisees' emphasis on laws.

Jesus was in a difficult situation. On the one hand, the laws of the Pharisees were based on God's Law; their legal furniture was stacked deep all over the foundation of the Ten Commandments. Jesus had no wish to violate God's Law. On the other hand, the Pharisees were far from understanding the personal reality of God and lacked the basic will to please Him. As all human beings, they could not keep God's Law. Their guilt was obvious. They wanted others to do what they, themselves, were unable to do—to please God by obeying laws. Jesus called these Pharisees whitewashed tombs filled with decaying bones.

TWO GREAT PRINCIPLES

Jesus did not see the Law of God as rules and regulations but as principles. He emphasized the two great principles that are basic. The Law of God and the teachings of the prophets—the whole Old Testament—make sense because of these two principles.

Jesus referred to one of these principles as "a new law." In their emphasis on law, the Pharisees had missed the crucial point. Jesus offered it as something they might add to their list. He knew very well it would stand out as being different. It was the principle of love! "A new commandment I give you: love one another" (John 13:34).

On another occasion He put both of the basic principles together. The first, He said, was already right in front of their noses as the first of the Ten Commandments: "Love the Lord your God with all your heart and with all your soul and with all your mind" (Matthew 22:37). The second principle, He said, was like the first, not lesser nor greater, not separable, not from some different source, but of the same value: "Love your neighbor as yourself" (Matthew 22:39).

When Jesus said that He did not come to abolish but to fulfill the Law (Matthew 5:17), He meant that instead of either discarding or expanding the Law, He came to draw attention to the underlying principles: love between God and human beings and love of people for each other. In these two, all the Law and the prophets hold together. (See Matthew 7:12 and 22:40.)

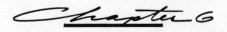

HOW CHILDREN SEE
RIGHT AND WRONG

I have had playmates, I have had companions,
In my days of childhood, in my joyful school days,—
All, all are gone; the old familiar faces.

Charles Lamb, *The Old Familiar Faces*

Alongside our sentimental memories of the happy times of childhood, most of us can remember bits and pieces of the other side of the story—the dog that bit, the bloody nose brought on by a difference of opinion about who was next at bat, the feeling that over and over again we had disappointed those we wanted most to please, and, underlying it all, so many things we didn't understand.

Rarely are children as snugly at peace with the world as poets suggest. Frightening mysteries abound—glimpses of adults at war with each other over things that don't make sense, unclear meanings, expectations that can't be met. New things are happening all the time, and even when adults listen to a child, they often don't understand.

Out of this confusion, a sense of right and wrong somehow emerges. To know what is right and what is wrong is part of the survival need of the child. It is no surprise that the notion of right and wrong has its first meaning for a child in self-centered terms. The child *feels* right and wrong. Only later does the child *know* right and wrong.

Childhood has its limitations. Perhaps an adult could grasp this more easily after spending a few hours sitting on the floor below the adult world of high tables and gigantic observers and seeing how things look from a child's perspective. Development is a matter of growing beyond such limitations. A more mature perspective, more experiences to build on, more complex uses of the mind for reasoning—these are the raw materials for the development of reasoning. "When I was a child, I talked like a child, I thought like a child, I reasoned like a child. When I became a man, I put childish ways behind me" (1 Corinthians 13:11).

What does it mean to think as a child? To reason as a child? It's not so much a lack of knowledge but a narrow viewpoint and a limited reasoning process. A child cannot think as an adult. Parents need to realize that a change in reasoning ability comes with maturation. Let's look at a child's view of life and his reasoning processes.

A CHILD'S VIEW	A CHILD'S REASONING
Self-centered universe.	What matters most is me.
Self-satisfying values.	What is important is how it affects me.
Sees others as things.	What is good for me is good for everybody.
Hears moral instruction only as commands.	I must keep testing the limits to find out what the rules are.
Sees morality being determined by rewards and punishments.	It's okay if you don't get caught.

The development of moral judgment is more complex than physical or mental development. Moral judgment is not something that simply grows when fed, nor can it be learned like facts of a subject in school. Moral judgment develops through a relationship between what the child learns about right and wrong as determined by others in the environment and what the child discovers about himself or herself as a person.

MORE THAN ENVIRONMENT

Environment doesn't account for everything. Two children can grow up side by side, having virtually the same experiences and engaging in similar relationships, only to turn out as two very different adults. What each child takes into account is distinctive. In these early connections between outside circumstances and personal feelings, the child shows a great deal of personality. What one child is sensitive to, another child will ignore. This difference reflects inherited factors of personality.

While parents set patterns or models for their children's moral judgments, each child builds his or her own structure. Parents can't pass it down; their example does not produce moral conscience in the child. Children copy parents' behaviors—at least to see how satisfying the actions may be. A child is apt to talk and act like the parents, whether or not the child believes in what he or she is saying and doing.

Frequent talking with and listening to a child has a valuable effect on moral development. Helping the child think and talk about intentions and consequences of actions is important, especially when the emphasis of the conversation is on the needs of others. A relationship of contract can be built between parents and child in which the child is "bargained" into meeting standards within his or her skills and abilities. This relationship, if based on respect and fairness, is useful in dealing with more serious misbehaviors of children and adolescents.

In the early 1920s, one of the first modern studies of moral education was conducted at Columbia University by

Hugh Hartshorne and Mark May. Their research findings are disturbing even today, especially since they found so little effect from "character education" programs of schools and churches. The research focused primarily on academic cheating and other forms of dishonesty. Hartshorne and May found that people can't be classified as honest or dishonest in any clear-cut way; almost everyone cheats in one way or another some of the time. They also found that dishonesty depends on the situation; a person will cheat in one situation but not in another. Among the most important findings are these:

● What people say about their moral values has little to do with how they act. This conclusion reminds us that verbal morality is almost useless. If the major goal of our moral teaching is to get children to say the right answers, we are deceiving ourselves. There's a big step from what a person says to what a person does.

● The tendency to be honest or dishonest varies according to the situation. Risk of detection, pressure of the "need to cheat," and the need for group approval are important in making a decision.

Parents should not be surprised at slips in a child's moral actions any more than they are with their own behavior. Parents should consider the degree of temptation that the child can handle. For example, the temptation to play with a pretty vase may be too great for a three-year-old, even if the child is aware of the wrongness of handling it. It's better to move the vase to a higher shelf. But don't count on the higher shelf as a long-term solution. The temptations mount far beyond any parent's ability to shield the child. Within a few years the whole world will open up to the child, and it will be full of temptations. It makes little difference whether the young person is within a "protected" home or Christian school. For example, consider the sometimes overwhelming pressure at high school and college level to get good grades in order to qualify for programs the parents have held up as ideal.

● Group approval is also a very powerful force that makes the child want to conform to a particular behavior. When everyone frowns at you, pretty soon you decide not to burp. But if everyone laughs when you burp, you try to do it more often. Are you visualizing a four-year-old at the dining table, or a half-sober man at a bar? Group approval is the shaping force in either situation.

The day-care facility is where peer choices begin for many children nowadays. Parents can encourage making friends with children from homes wherein respectable values are honored. Choices of playmates and friends cannot be controlled, but they can and should be encouraged.

On the other hand, some contact with children whose values are destructive is inevitable and, in measured doses, can be stimulating to the social development process. Much depends on the sort of communicative relationship between the child and the parents. Children have many potentially negative experiences that can be turned to the positive with the right sort of talking through with the parents.

MENTAL DEVELOPMENT

Much of what we know about the process of mental development has come from the studies of Jean Piaget (pronounced Zhahn Pee-ah-ZHAY). This remarkable Swiss psychologist spent his whole life studying children. His major interest was in how children think. To determine this, he used one of the basic methods of social science: watching.

In his home city, Geneva, Piaget observed children in all sorts of situations—at play, at school, at home. He listened closely to how children talk to each other, how they talk to adults, and even how they talk to themselves.

Jean Piaget encourages us to see a child as a child, not as a miniature or immature adult. A child thinks differently from an adult. A normal adult has developed mental processes that are not available to a child. The child can and does think, but he does it in ways that the adult has long forgotten. The adult who expects a child to come close to his way of looking at things is apt to be very frustrated and, in turn, to make life very miserable for the child.

A small child is unable to see things from any point of view but his own. A lack of intelligence is not the issue; the child simply is locked into one viewpoint or perspective. Because of this, a child has trouble being concerned about other people's feelings.

When an adult does or says something that hurts another's feelings, we can be sure that either the act is intentional or that the adult is careless. We would likely say that the adult is cruel or insensitive. On the other hand, when a seven-year-old does or says something that hurts our feelings, we should not interpret it as cruel or insensitive behavior. Indeed it may hurt, but the child cares about his own feelings, not someone else's. (Sometimes adults still act like children in this respect, but it's usually because they choose to think in self-centered ways.)

Since the child lacks perspective, should parents try to do something about it? Piaget's research shows that whatever you do, whatever you say, and no matter how you push, the child still has a child's view of life.

In other words, viewpoint is not a matter of information alone. Surely you can teach the child facts. But it is far more important to show him that there are other viewpoints. The child can't use facts to reason with until he can mentally transport himself into someone else's shoes. And arriving at this sort of maturity takes time.

What sort of understanding would the child have of such an idea as the Golden Rule, "Do unto others what you would have them do unto you"? This distinction between self and

others is not made in the reasoning processes of the pre-
schooler. Thus the Rule will have very limited meaning; more
than likely it will get turned around to the simpler idea that if
someone does something to hurt me, I should hurt that
person in return. The child is clear enough about what he
wants from others, but is not yet able to connect that idea to
the need to do good for others.

Younger children are limited to seeing a moral world in
self-centered terms. Good is what feels good or works out to
one's own advantage. Bad is what feels bad or works out to
one's hurt. The distinction between right and wrong is largely
limited to these simple notions of personal feeling. Parents
ordinarily start early to say, "Bobby, that's a no-no." "Arlie,
that's not nice . . . not right . . . we don't do that . . . that's
bad." And on it goes, having little effect on moral understanding, but still very necessary—at least for developing the basic
vocabulary of moral communication.

The child must learn to associate these words—*no, not
nice, bad, wrong,* and *don't*—with some sort of *real* or concrete result of having done the thing. Since the child's mind
focuses on the concrete, the words will have little meaning
and no effect until they are attached predictably to a negative
or hurtful outcome. This relation must be made in the child's
own mind, and it can't be made *for* him, no matter how much
the parent may try. Moral conscience comes through the
child's own experiences.

Few things are more important in a child's early development than having people around who are consistent. So long
as the parent is gentle, almost anything done consistently to
help the child find the difference between good and bad behavior will be useful. There are few magic formulas for bringing
up children—but being as consistent as possible is perhaps the
closest. Too much inconsistency is likely to retard the child's
moral development.

The day will come when the child discovers the difference between right and wrong. Yes, surely he has been told the difference, but that is only one part of the process. The learning occurs when the child sees in his own actions the possibility of predicting good and bad effects.

Even a small child will begin to look around sheepishly just before or after doing a "no-no." Some children may *do* the wrong action while *saying* the right choice. A little girl may invade the refrigerator and eat something while saying "no-no." The child knows the *no* but is not strong enough to resist temptation. In such a moment you can see the first traces of moral conscience. It is marvelous to watch, and often humorous. But if adults laugh about the child's little "badness," the child becomes confused and is likely to be set back. Employ too much of scold-one-time-and-laugh-the-next, and you will have a morally underdeveloped child on your hands.

One other word of caution. The child is not a puppy to be trained. God has created us with a remarkable moral sensitivity. A steady schedule of rewards and punishments isn't needed to awaken it. Gentle, loving consistency is the human way.

Chapter 7

KNOWING WHY

Have you ever taken a good look at your moral values? You know that some things are right and other things are wrong. You pay attention to these values as you go through your day. But have you ever taken a close look? For example, did you ever write a list of the kinds of decisions you tend to make and the behaviors that are typical of your life? It would be a good exercise.

Beyond this, do you have any idea why you believe your decisions and behaviors are important? What are the deep roots of your view of good and evil? Perhaps the next few chapters will help you get better acquainted with yourself.

The concern for values, especially moral values and ethics, is as old as mankind. In every era of human history, laws, rules, ethical codes, and other matters of moral behavior have been talked about, debated, and passed down through oral tradition. In literate societies, statements of moral values were among the earliest writings.

There is no evidence of God having given a written record until the time of Moses. At Mount Sinai God inscribed the Law on panels of stone. Thus began Moses' great task of writing down the history of God's people.

Moses is recognized both as the lawgiver and as the author of the Pentateuch. Under the inspiration of the Holy Spirit of God, he wrote down all of the vital experiences from the Garden of Eden until the entry of the Children of Israel into the Promised Land.

The writings of the great philosophers have focused on moral issues and the problem of determining what is good. The ethicists and moralists of all traditions are, as a whole, concerned with matters of good and evil, right and wrong. But all of these studies emphasize the *content* of moral judgment. Placing exclusive emphasis on content tends toward dangerous oversimplifications:

• Assuming that being moral is simply a matter of knowing what is right;

• Assuming that developing morally is a matter of learning more rules;

• Assuming that human beings can learn their way into higher moral standards.

People who make these errors will buy into almost any scheme that gives people the right moral answers and then punishes them for disobedience. Whenever I hear someone say, "But I told you not to!" I am reminded that *being told* is not enough. When I say to myself, "I knew better than to do that," I am reminded that *knowing* is not enough. Indeed, when I think of the patience God shows as He instructs, forgives, corrects, and encourages us, I realize that knowing what God has said is only one small part of being a moral person.

MORAL REASONING

In recent years increased attention has been given to the *structure* of moral judgment. Many research studies have expanded our understanding of moral judgment and the way it develops.

The favorite research procedure for these studies is the interview. Those who think of scientists as people in white coats who hold smoking test tubes and stopwatches may have a hard time with this fact. Social scientists spend most of their time listening to people.

The newer research is concerned not only with *what* people believe but with *why* they believe it. Don't be too critical of this shifted emphasis; no one is suggesting that *what* you believe is unimportant! If you understand the structure of moral judgment, you are better able to help people with the difficult task of decisively acting on what they believe.

It's wrong to steal. Why? Because it's wrong to hurt people. Why? Because it's good to love people. Why? Because it's good to do what Jesus tells us. Why?

Does this sound like a conversation between a small boy and his mother? Perhaps. It could also be a conversation between you and me. I would have asked first, "What things do you think of as *wrong*, and what things do you think of as *good?*" Then, no matter what your answers, one by one I would have asked, "Why?" You would be participating in some of the most interesting research of the last decade. Throughout the world but especially in the United States, England, and Canada, social scientists have been asking these questions: What do you value? Why do you value it? Why are certain kinds of behavior called *good* while others are labeled *bad?*

The research scientists have been more interested in the Why than in the What. The reason is plain. So much attention has been given to the content of moral issues by moral philosophers and religious writers. Now the rest of the matter is being opened up.

Growing up involves changes in one's moral judgment. However, most people would recall that since their earliest memories they have known it is right or wrong to do certain things. Does this mean that there has been little development?

No. It means that two kinds of change are involved in moral development.

Consider first the content of a moral value. This aspect is easiest to identify because it is what most people mean when they refer to moral development. What one believes to be right and wrong is the *content* of one's value system.

Why the concern here for the technical vocabulary? Because with this basic distinction between two aspects of moral judgment you see more about what moral development is. You understand better your own experience as a valuing person. Also, you understand how a person develops morally.

You need only to be able to make the distinction between content and structure. Try to remember it this way: *content* is the *what* of a moral judgment; *structure* is the *why* of a moral judgment.

When you say, "Stealing is wrong," you likely have a reason for saying so. Sometimes these reasons are called beliefs. They may or may not relate to religious beliefs. Psychologists call these reasons *structure*.

The structure of a moral judgment is the *why* that causes you to hold to the content of the judgment. *What* you believe to be right or wrong is the content. Why you believe it to be right or wrong is the structure.

Think of the structure of a belief as the framework under a bridge. The surface of the bridge carries the load of the traffic. Underneath is what makes it hold firm—the structure.

When I was a boy, a railroad ran across the end of a lake near where we lived. It was such fun standing at the shore of that lake watching the trains pass high above. They rattled the track, the wooden trestle and, it seemed, the whole earth.

Then World War II started and the railroad was regarded as an important target for sabotage. Day after day we watched as carloads of gravel and dirt were dumped through and around the trestle, filling that part of the lake to make a new base of solid earth under the tracks. The old structure was replaced by a new one. The track stayed the same, and the railroad service was not disrupted during the change.

What happens in moral development is much like that. The development of structure may mean a complete change of what lies underneath a moral value, but becoming mature requires the change. The old structure was part of childhood. The new structure reflects the more thorough thought and understanding that mental and social growth bring.

At one level of development a person may be structurally guided by what others will say or expect. At another level of development, the person's structure may be dominated by a commitment to the orderliness that rules and laws bring about. Very likely the content of the person's values hasn't changed much during this time. For example, the person may still hold exactly the same position about the wrongness of lying, stealing, cheating, or whatever. The difference is that he or she has a new way of thinking about the moral wrongness and a new mental process to use in making judgments.

Earlier, this person was thinking, "It's wrong to steal because the people who are important in my life will be disappointed or displeased if I steal." Later, the person's thoughts might be, "It's wrong to steal because there are rules and laws against stealing. If I break these laws, I won't be doing my part to create the kind of orderly world I want to live in."

Consider the matter of obeying God. Even a small child can learn what God wants him to do. Why would the child want to obey God? God is our Heavenly Father and does good things for His children. Or, God is powerful and dangerous and punishes those who disobey Him. Indeed, both of these ideas are biblical and both are understandable, even to small children. So which will it be?

Those who influence the child determine which emphasis the child will see most clearly; on this base the child's structure of belief about obeying God begins to form. "I want to obey God because He is my Heavenly Father; I want Him to do good things for me." Or, "I want to obey God because He will punish me if I don't."

At any level of moral development there are varieties of structure. We are not all alike. Even on the matters of content where we agree, we might disagree about why we agree.

THE PROCESS OF MORAL JUDGMENT

Moral judgment is the mental process by which we decide that a given thing is good or evil. The following interview illustrates how the content and structure of a moral decision become that process.

"Did you cheat on the spelling test this morning?"

"No."

"Why not?"

"It's wrong to cheat."

"What does someone do when he or she cheats on a test?"

"Copies, I guess. Or looks up the answers. Maybe you get somebody to help you."

"Is that wrong?"

"Yes, on a test it's wrong."

"How do you know it's wrong."

"The teacher said not to."

"Is what the teacher said important?"

"Yes."

"Why?"

"Because the teacher makes the rules."

"Would it be all right to cheat on the test if the teacher didn't say anything about it?"

"No."

"Why not?"

"Cheating is always wrong."

"What is cheating?"

"When you don't do what's right. When you say you did something yourself and you really didn't."

"What other words can you use for cheating?"

"Maybe dishonesty. Maybe stealing."

"In what way is it like stealing or dishonesty?"

"People who cheat are stealing good grades. That's not honest."

"Why is that wrong?"

"You get in trouble when you're dishonest."

"What do you mean?"

"Your mother or somebody will punish you."

"Are you ever dishonest?"

"Sometimes."

"How does that make you feel?"

"It makes me afraid. I don't like it."

"Why not?"

"I don't like to get punished."

Notice how the interview alternates between *what* questions and *why* questions, going deeper and deeper into the structure that lies behind the content that cheating is wrong. The first hint of moral structure is in these words, "The teacher said not to." The interview continues, but the further it goes the clearer it is that this person thinks of cheating this way:

Content: Cheating is wrong. It is a form of stealing. It is not honest.

Structure: Cheating is wrong because you are likely to be punished for it. The teacher (or possibly another person in authority) determines the rightness or wrongness of the act and has the responsibility to punish violations.

As children mature, they will need to go back over the same Bible stories and teachings several different times. This kind of mental recycling is very important if new and more mature moral structure is to be attached to the stories and lessons. For those who do not get this sort of experience, the result in adulthood is only childish associations and meanings of virtually all of the Bible materials that they were ever taught. For example, Samson is a vivid story for a child. It is likely to stick with the youngster throughout life. When it is first learned, it is almost surely heard as a good-guys-and-bad-guys story in which the bad guys hurt the good guy, but sooner or later the good guy gets his chance to kill the bad guys. (What a lovely moral lesson to carry through life.)

Such stories must be revisited through the process of growing up in order to add texture, detail, dimension, and most important, moral maturity, so that the facts of Samson's sinfulness and God's righteousness can be brought into focus. Ultimately the lesson must be understood in terms of sin and its consequences alongside of God's righteousness and the assurance that His justice ultimately rules the universe. While this view is hardly within the grasp of a four-year-old, that age is not too young to begin dealing with the story of Samson.

Wise parents and properly planned programs of religious education will employ this procedure of the cyclical return to material taught earlier—sometimes called a *spiral curriculum*—paying special attention to the structure in the young person's moral reasoning. The point of a spiral curriculum is not just to make sure that all the details get told, but far more important, to encourage the learner to rethink the meaning of the story at a more mature level of moral structure.

Think about how you would have responded to the interview questions. Before you read the next chapter, look at the *what* and *why* of your own values. When you have learned to think about both content and structure, you are better able to understand the process of moral judgment.

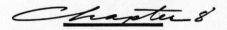

THE BASIS FOR STRUCTURAL DEVELOPMENT

In what ways do people grow up? Physically, they get larger and stronger and become much more able to use the body in athletic and expressive ways. Sexual characteristics and capabilities emerge all in a rather predictable sequence.

Emotionally, people become more complex as sensitivities and awarenesses develop, and they become capable of response to a wider array of emotional situations. They develop unique personalities, largely a reflection of the complex variety of their emotional characteristics. Emotional maturity suggests the capability of coping with life. The older one gets the more one is exposed to difficult emotional challenges. Being young and dependent provides an emotional shield. Growing up pulls away this shield so that one must deal with more demanding pressures.

When the responsibilities of parenthood are added, the tests become severe. The ability to handle the emotional challenges of adulthood is an area in which many people need help.

SOCIAL DEVELOPMENT

Growing up socially means accepting the increasing responsibilities of relationships with other people. Small children can't play together very long without hitting one another. Older children tend to hurt each other with words. Their social relationships need to be supervised.

Growing up socially means going through more or less predictable stages. First one gains an awareness that other people are real and that they too have feelings and a sense of property. Following this is a series of skill-development tasks in which the person finds ways to enhance his or her own pleasure and security by relating in certain ways to others. Then comes a more genuine concern for the well-being of others and the development of the skills of kindness.

MENTAL DEVELOPMENT

Mental development is closely related to all other kinds of growth. A person's mental capabilities emerge in a predictable sequence. While everyone does not develop at the same rate, most people move through the same stages. Jean Piaget has identified four mental development stages.

● The Sensorimotor Stage begins at birth (some say before). The child enters life with a great deal of dependence on simple senses. Most of the clues the infant gets about the environment come from hitting, kicking, or bumping into things. This limited early learning is one of the distinctive features of being human. Most behavior is very simple reaction—a sudden noise might cause a jerking reaction followed by crying; closeness of mother or a bottle of warm milk might start the sucking noises. But whatever learning is taking place is very simple. It might be better explained as getting ready to learn.

● In the Preoperational Stage, the child still cannot use his mind for any complex thinking. Thoughts are limited to his own experience. Although language skills are developing rapidly in this period, he can think of only one idea at a time, and the relationship between cause and effect is beyond his understanding.

● Next is the Concrete Operational Stage. In this stage of development, children (and adults too, because not everyone goes significantly beyond this stage) develop useful, logical ways to relate to things and to people. One learns to identify, analyze, and categorize. Telling the difference between a robin and a bluejay is no problem at all. How to put oneself to work, how to convert labor into money, and how to convert money into material possessions are easy uses of the mind in this stage.

● The highest level of mental development is what Piaget calls the Formal Operational Stage. When the person has reached this level, the mind can be used as a formal logic-processing device. In other words, no matter how abstract the idea, the mind can grasp it and "operate" on it. Abstract questions such as "Who am I?" "What is the purpose of life?" "What is truth?" demand formal operations. (From *The Origins of Intelligence in Children*, International Universities Press, 1952.)

Moral development and mental development are not the same; but until a person's mental development has moved forward, moral development will not proceed either. As we will see in the next chapter, moral development and mental development both require some of the same learning experiences.

The chart on stages of mental development shows some of the questions and answers that reveal the differences in the way people think at each stage. There are no ages on the chart because people develop at different rates. The minute that parents see an age specified, they check to see if their child is "normal," or, better yet, "ahead of normal." Fretting about what to do to make kids fit the pattern is actually dangerous.

From the list, you can see the shifts that occur from stage to stage. As a matter of fact, this list represents the same boy at three different times in his life. From your own experiences with children, can you estimate his age at the time of the first two interviews? He was twenty at the time of the last interview.

The differences between Stages 2 and 3 are much less important to the matter of values and moral judgment than the contrast between Stages 3 and 4. Although some of the responses in the Stage 4 column aren't particularly precise, we can see that Bill is now thinking about issues. Life is not quite so black and white anymore. This ability to deal with abstract concepts is necessary for the higher forms of moral judgment. But how does all of this relate to moral development?

MORAL DEVELOPMENT

Lawrence Kohlberg of Harvard University directed a series of research studies into the moral reasoning of a group of boys and men as they developed over a period of nearly twenty years. Taking his inspiration from Piaget's search for stages of intellectual development, Kohlberg looked for evidence of a pattern in the development of moral reasoning within the subjects of his research. He found a small amount of predictable change in the content of moral development. But what little evidence there is for predictable changes in moral *content* is overshadowed by strong evidence that the *structure* of moral judgment develops in predictable patterns.

Kohlberg found that moral judgment emerges through three distinct levels. The three levels of moral judgment are most important. Knowing about them helps us to understand ourselves better. They give us a much clearer idea of what the educational and parental tasks really are.

For the Christian, there is special encouragement in Kohlberg's findings. His research agrees remarkably well with

RESPONSES ILLUSTRATING THE THREE UPPER STAGES OF MENTAL DEVELOPMENT

Interview QUESTIONS	Stage 2: PREOP-ERATIONAL	Stage 3: CONCRETE OPERATIONS	Stage 4: FORMAL OPERATIONS
1. Who are you?	Billy.	William H. Smith, Junior.	I'm still trying to find out!
2. Where do you live?	In a house.	In Dalton, Georgia.	I live *anywhere*, friend.
3. Do you sing?	Sure—want to hear me? Lah, lah, lee, lah, lah.	Do I sing *what?*	Yes (or No).
4. Who is your daddy (or father)?	Him (pointing).	Mr. Smith.	In what sense?
5. Are you a "doubting Thomas"?	What?	No.	Sometimes.
6. What's the most important day in your life?	Christmas.	My birthday.	The day when I found . . . (or discovered, began to see . . . , or entered a particular relationship).
7. Is friendship important to you?	Yep . . . what?	At least with Bobby and Joe, maybe Arlene too.	Oh, yes, very important.
8. Where can you learn about the purpose of life?	What?	In books.	Each person must find it for himself.
9. What is truth?	Not telling a lie.	Telling what is right.	It's hard to define, but truth is a sort of principle you believe in.

what the Bible teaches about childhood, about unredeemed man, and about moral and spiritual development. However, since he did not claim any Christian beliefs for himself, the way Kohlberg dealt with a person's relationship to *authority*, the question of *obedience*, and the *source* of moral good differs from what many Christians believe. Nonetheless, we can be thankful that the research frontier has been expanded. The new insights are helpful for Christians.

Kohlberg found that three different kinds of structure account for virtually all moral judgments. (From "Development of Moral Character and Moral Ideology," *Review of Child Development Research*, Vol. 1, Russell Sage Foundation, 1964).

Level I, *preconventional judgment,* focuses on me and my concerns. "Good" is what serves my purposes and makes me feel good about something. "Bad" or "wrong" is what hurts me or my own interests. Punishment and reward are the major influences toward moral good. Billy says, "I know it's wrong because every time I do it, I get in trouble."

Level II, *conventional judgment,* focuses on other people. Moral judgments are made on the basis of concerns outside oneself. Early in this level, the way to determine right and wrong depends on what pleases or displeases the people who are important to me. Later in this level, I realize that rules and regulations are the highest form of clear statements about right and wrong. Examples and rules are the major influences toward moral good. Billy says, "I don't do that because Jesus wouldn't do it."

Level III, *postconventional judgment,* focuses on principles. Moral judgments are made on the basis of principles, especially the principles that underlie the behavior I value in myself and others. Billy says, "I don't even want to do that because it wouldn't be consistent with what God is doing within me."

Everyone starts in the first level. As the child begins to have a moral awareness or conscience and to make moral judgments, the first level is always the one that accounts for the judgment process.

Then as moral judgment develops, we pass from the first to the second and then to the third structural level. The order is a predictable sequence. You can still make judgments of the first level sort, but development may have released you into one of the more mature levels.

But not everyone moves from level to level. Many people stay in the first level. Some adults still use first level moral judgment. Even more people remain in the second level. The second level is especially comfortable if you crave order and accept authority. You might even be happy to remain there. But if you can't accept order and authority, you might go through life in Level I with only yourself as guide.

As we move into higher levels of moral judgment, we do not forget how to make decisions on the simpler level. Instead, we add the new structure to the possible ways of looking at a moral issue. Remember the illustration of the new structure of dirt and gravel for the timber railroad trestle? The new structure became the dominant one, but the old structure was still there, deep inside.

Kohlberg found that at any level, a person can understand moral messages which are tuned to his or her level and that appeal to the structure of that level. When you hear a moral message that is over your head, do you try to bring it down to your level? If so, you may be distorting it.

Kohlberg also discovered that religious conversion has a minimal effect on one's moral judgment. This point causes some Christians to see a red flag. Surely one's religious experience has some positive effect on moral judgment. But where in the Bible are we promised instant maturity?

Yes, in Christ "the new has come" (2 Corinthians 5:17),

but this "new creature," made new by spiritual regeneration, must then enter into a lifelong process of maturing according to the processes described extensively in the New Testament literature.

Our *relationship* to God and God's view of us change instantly through religious conversion. God begins a good work in us (Philippians 1:6). That work of the Holy Spirit is a long and steady process that takes a lifetime. This process is a matter of cooperation with our own will to work with God (Philippians 2:12-13). If it were a matter of instant *maturity,* why did Peter emphasize growing? (1 Peter 2:1-3 and 2 Peter 3:17-18)

We need to remember what conversion does and doesn't do. Who among us no longer sins? Who among us claims always to do what is right? Who has completed the moral development process and can smoothly glide through life? We must keep on throwing off "everything that hinders, and the sin that so easily entangles, and . . . run with perseverance the race marked out for us" (Hebrews 12:1).

In his research, Kohlberg dealt mainly with moral judgment; he was only slightly concerned about moral action. God is concerned primarily with moral action (obedience) and, therefore, God is also concerned with moral judgment. The Christian is concerned with both moral judgment and moral action. A moral act has moral consequences and depends on moral judgment. Our moral actions can be no better than our moral judgments.

Consider the difference between rules and principles. Rules are external. They are the voices of others—of society, of my nation, of God. But principles are internal. I can't bring rules in because they belong to the outside; but I *can* bring principles in. Principles are what I have selected and brought in from what I respect and value. If God's Law means rules and regulations, it is outside me. But if God's Law means principles, it can come inside and transform me.

God wants His people to be changed on the *inside*. God prefers that His Law be written inside on the heart rather than just inscribed on tablets of stone (2 Corinthians 3:3). This contrast suggests the distinction between responding to the external Law and changing inside by building one's life on internal moral convictions.

Jesus did not come to destroy the Law but to fulfill it (Matthew 5:17). In fulfilling the Law, He respected it. But He also demonstrated the two principles that underlie all of God's Laws: love for God and love for other people. The Law is a tutor that brings us to Christ (Galatians 3:24). The Law can't live within us, but Christ can!

For the Christian, the key to life and to development is love. The Apostle Paul listed virtues and spiritual gifts one by one and said that each was worthless without love (1 Corinthians 13). Jesus offered a new commandment to His disciples: that they should love one another (John 13:34). A commandment to love? The *principle* of love gives meaning to the Bible. Love is the basic principle for the Christian's moral value judgments.

Chapter 9

HOW *WHY* DEVELOPS

Why? Mommy, why?" Parents can grow weary of this question. Children ask "Why?" partly because they discover that it is a good way to stall for time and partly because they really want to know. They will ask until they are turned off, temporarily or permanently.

Why is a very human question. When you ask it, you are making an important claim on being a person. *Why* shows belief in purpose. *Why* says that you want to share anything that anyone else knows about what lies beyond the obvious. *Why* shows self-respect: you believe that you are capable of understanding.

"Daddy, why are there clouds? Daddy, why is the dog barking? Daddy, why must I go to bed?" Whether the question can be answered with scientific facts, personal opinions, or concrete reasons, *why* helps people get together. It provides a good basis for sharing experiences.

Mental and moral development do not depend on storing lots of good answers in your memory but on learning to ask important questions. Real development means recognizing issues and seeing what needs to be explored. It also means committing yourself to using your understanding to solve the problems that confront you.

FOUR FACTORS IN MENTAL DEVELOPMENT

To better understand how the moral judgment process develops, let's look at the factors involved in mental development—the overall process of which moral judgment is surely one part. Again we turn to the research of Jean Piaget, who found four factors that account for mental development. Each of us as parents and as individuals can gain self-understanding and perhaps learn more about relating to others from the study of these points.

• Heredity and maturation. The child has inherited the genetic material of mankind. The patterns of development are built into each person. Of course, what is built in is only a broad outline of when and how certain growth will occur. The normal child will grow taller, but how tall?

In the mental realm, the child will develop capabilities for abstract thoughts and artistic creativity. Just how strong will these capabilities be? To what extent will the abilities be used? For these answers we must look to the other three factors. Genetic emergence (heredity) is important to development, but is not something that we can control.

• Experience. Our knowledge and understanding are based on our own experience, which plays a very important part in development. Parents should be concerned with providing for the child a variety and depth of experiences, many of which are shared with the rest of the family. If the experiences of parents and children have very little overlap, the family will lack unity.

In the sense used here, experience is concerned with *doing*, not just watching or listening. Especially in the younger child, active play and sports are important. Through doing things *in* the world and doing things *to* the world, we develop understanding of that world.

Largely because of television's power to fascinate *and deactivate* children, the current generation is lacking in first-hand experience. Today's children are informed, perhaps even a bit better informed than children were before television; but today's diet of spectator sports, observer activities, and nonparticipative loneliness do not add up to adequate experience of the sort that stimulates creativity, craft skills, and musical and artistic expression in developing youngsters.

The world that you know best is the world you construct in your own mind. The reality that counts is the reality of your own perceptions. Only through a wide variety of extensive experience can perception grow into a thorough grasp of life.

● Social transaction. In the animal realm, social development involves doing exactly what other creatures of that species do. Behaviors of "family" members blend together because the range of tasks and roles is very small.

Human development is different because the range of possible human activities is vast. As we develop, we become not more alike but more different in highly specialized ways. These differences would cause people to become more estranged and isolated if it were not for the socialization process.

Through socialization or becoming a more social, interdependent person, we develop behaviors and outlooks similar to those of people around us. In these social experiences, we are affected as much by what *we do to others* as by what *they do to us*. In other words, we are not shaped or molded as if we were lumps of clay.

We can compare social interaction to catching and throwing a ball. Muscles are strengthened not because of what the ball does but because of what the person does to the ball. With this in mind, it is easier to see why the same experience has different effects on different people.

As we relate to other people, we are affected by the process. What we do and say within a relationship has its effects on our understanding and on our interpersonal skills. Thus we can see how one good experience leads to another—and also how one bad experience is apt to lead to another.

All of us, including children, need many opportunities for contacts with other people. Through these social encounters our self-understanding develops. We discover the relationships that are constructive and effective.

● Equilibration. Life is full of experiences that don't quite fit into our normal patterns. When these little surprises come along, the bumps and swerves are not always comfortable. But if everything in life were easy and predictable, not much growth would result. Much of our development depends on stretching open our viewpoints to assimilate new ideas. Often, we need to change the shape of our understanding in order to accommodate facts and impressions that don't quite fit the old molds.

Even as a bicycle rider leans and sways, the developing person is pushed from side to side in his thinking. Riding a bicycle isn't a matter of keeping it rock-solid steady. It's a matter of gaining and losing equilibrium. On each stroke of the pedals, disequilibration (going somewhat off-balance) is necessary to continue riding. Disequilibration is also an essential part of human development. As a person encounters events and ideas that don't quite fit together within present understandings, something has to give way. This may mean revising the whole reasoning system or structure of moral thought. This need for rethinking is one of the most important forces toward development of a higher structure.

Development of understanding and judgment is thus pushed forward. An experience pushes us, threatening our balance; we pull back, trying to find a new balance point. Then another unpredicted experience comes along, and the process continues. The tendency of the normal human is to find some way to regain stability and to develop *because of* the jolts and surprises.

Sometimes our concern for others causes us to protect them from every rough spot in life. To do so risks slowing down their development. We shouldn't try to create problems for each other. But we need to see the importance of each person dealing with life firsthand. Did you ever try to ride a bicycle for someone else? Worse yet, picture a father running alongside the bicycle while his son pedals—the father never quite letting go, the son never quite learning.

FOUR FACTORS IN MORAL DEVELOPMENT

Moral judgment develops through almost the same processes. Lawrence Kohlberg has identified four factors that contribute to the development of moral judgment.

● Experiences of justice. Susan had never understood justice. Then one day she and her classmates played a game in which the opportunity to win depended on having dark hair. Susan became angry because she saw how unfair it was to be a loser because of her blonde hair. She learned the difference between justice and injustice.

We learn much about morality from the moral environment in which we spend our time. People who are treated fairly usually develop faster than those who experience constant injustice. If we are respected, we discover the value of respect and tend to treat others that way. If we are treated with fairness and honesty, we tend to treat others in the same manner. But if we are treated unfairly and dishonestly, we will be more likely to show the same unfairness to others. Adults who take advantage of others and justify themselves on the basis of race, social status, or wealth are morally immature. The reason for such immaturity may very well be traced to having been reared in an unjust environment.

Nothing has more influence on the development of moral

judgment than participation in a just environment. But our view of justice changes as development occurs. To a child in the first level of development, justice has a self-centered meaning. It means not doing more than one's own share. It also means being allowed to do what someone else is doing.

During this time, the older family members need patience and understanding as the child begins to knowingly ask and answer questions about fairness. The time invested in bridging the gap between the child's view and the adult's view is not wasted. Rather, it is a small price to pay in helping the child grasp the real meaning of justice.

● Experiences of social interaction. Social experience has much to do with moral development. People who avoid contacts with others are likely to develop more slowly. We gain in moral judgment as we become more familiar with other perspectives. If you had never encountered other viewpoints, you would likely think of your own as the only possible opinion, but you would have had no experience in defending it or even explaining it.

Some well-intentioned parents slow their children by keeping them well insulated from other children who might be a bad influence on them. It is important for any of us, children or adults, to be concerned about the company we keep. But to some extent we *need* to experience different viewpoints, including differences in moral convictions.

For example, whatever positive values may come from being in Christian schools throughout childhood, children need to encounter a wider variety of values and viewpoints. Without reasonable breadth of experience, a child rarely gains any depth of conviction; the child tends to assume that his views are everyone's views.

Until Bobby met Roger, it never occurred to him that throwing rocks through windows in the vacant house could be such fun. But when Roger hid from passersby, Bobby began to wonder. Later he asked his mother, "Why is Roger afraid of people?" That question opened up a deeper understanding of Roger and also of himself. Without the shock of the experience with Roger, Bobby would have missed an important learning opportunity.

• Open discussions of moral concerns. "It's wrong because I say so, and let's don't hear any more of it." This statement is one of the surest ways to retard moral judgment.

God has given us a marvelous capacity for communication. Using language well is one of the great open doors of development. Moral conscience is a natural tendency; but moral judgment depends on sharpening one's awareness and sharing ideas about meaning. This sharing takes place through discussion.

We should encourage each other to think and talk about the moral implications of the experiences around us. Under no circumstances should a child be turned off when he or she wants to talk about why something is right or wrong. Instead, every member of the family should work toward making it easy to ask questions honestly. A family environment that allows for open exchange of ideas will help in everyone's moral development, not just the children's.

Bobby's mother knew better than to scold for the window-breaking. She valued the fact that Bobby had come to her with his moral concern. She made it easy for him to talk about it.

• Opportunities for role playing. A person is many things: a daughter or son, a sister or brother, a mother or father, and perhaps a gardener, baker, driver, doctor, salesperson, and more. Can you recall your childhood role-playing experiences? You drove bulldozers, flew airplanes, acted on the stage, played traffic cop, teacher, football star, music director, and photographer. You tried on all sorts of roles.

Through role playing, we begin to search out a place for ourselves as grown-ups. But we also are discovering ourselves and thus gaining a basis for understanding others. The more experience we have in taking on the roles of others, the further our moral development is stimulated.

Every week or so Jill discovers something new about herself. Most of these discoveries come while she is "trying on" a new role. In the attic is a box of old clothes; in the garage, some small tools. Jill and her brothers play house, store, farm, highway repair, and dozens of other do-it-yourself situations. Even more important, Jill has discovered that she is a daughter, a sister, and a friend. She is learning to appreciate Jill.

Through family experiences in role playing, including the discovery of consequences of actions taken in the roles, a child develops the sense of responsibility which is a basic part of moral development.

THE TASK OF PARENTS

Christian parents know that they should be involved in the moral development of their children. The question is, How to help? Some things will do more harm than good. The moral influence of a parent is a complicated matter.

Effective discipline involves the parent in some act, short of forcefully controlling the child, that has a positive effect on the child's self-responsibility. At best, discipline should have positive moral influence. The approach to discipline needs to vary according to the child's level of moral judgment.

Children need encouragement and correction. In the years when moral judgment is only partially formed, a child needs reminders and coaching, lest the childish behavior become seriously antisocial and destructive. How can parents exert moral influence? Rewards and punishments have their place. Use them sparingly, with consistency, and with gentle kindness, or they will lose their effectiveness.

Later on, behavior problems are more likely to come from gaps between moral judgment and moral action. How can parents exert a positive effect on the moral actions of the maturing child? Rewards and punishments are useful in early years. As the child matures, consistent examples, models, and fair rules are more effective.

As moral judgment begins to develop in the child, it is highly ego-based. What is right is what feels right; what is wrong is what works to the child's hurt or disadvantage. In this period, rewards and punishments have their greatest effects in communicating moral influence.

When the child gains enough mental capability to grasp other people's viewpoints, the focus of moral judgment moves outside the self, and *others* become important as the source of moral authority. At this time the child becomes less responsive to rewards and punishments and more influenced by models and examples. In this second level of moral judgment, the orderliness that comes through rules and regulations becomes important. The developing person, usually adolescent or adult by now, responds to clearly defined and just rules.

Those who reach a principled-justice level of moral judgment, Kohlberg's Level III, lose some of their responsiveness to the moral influence of models and rules. Transactions and dialogues with other people become more important as a mode of moral influence.

KINDS OF MORAL DEVELOPMENT

Following is a chart of the strong moral influences at each level of moral development. The three levels are represented as zones or periods when each of the three major modes of moral influence are predicted to have their greatest influence. The first mode, rewards and punishments, relates best to people who are making moral judgments in terms of Level I. In Level II, models and rules are most effective. The third mode, dialogue and interpersonal transaction, is most effective for people who are in Level III.

THE STRONG MORAL INFLUENCES AT EACH LEVEL OF MORAL JUDGMENT

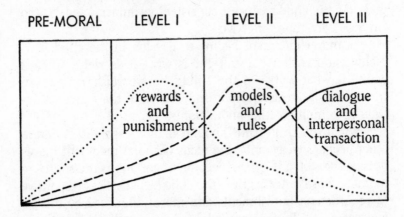

Several practical implications can be seen here. For example, who would be expected to respond best to a Sunday School attendance contest with its typical payoffs? Who is apt to be least influenced by a discussion of the moral implications of honesty? Who is most likely to be disinterested in a memory verse chart with gold and silver stars? Who is most apt to be influenced by an exciting biography or thrilling testimony? Who is most likely to be watching the example you set as you live?

Considering moral judgment in terms of religious development, who is most inclined to respond to threats of God's wrath? Who is most concerned about doing what Jesus would do? Who is most satisfied that "if God has said so, that settles it"? Who is most enthusiastic about daily fellowship with God, willingly and eagerly entered into?

VERTICAL INTEGRATION

In order that a mode of moral influence be available to the child when needed, it must be "phased in." We don't suddenly turn off one mode and turn on the next. For example, dialogue may not have much influence for the small child, but it should begin early in life.

The chart does not suggest that we lose our ability to respond to any of the earlier modes of moral influence. For example, even mature people are alert to the threat of punishment. Developing from level to level of moral reasoning does *not* mean that one *leaves* the reasoning typical of the lower level. Even before Kohlberg's more detailed findings, Piaget had called this process of bringing it all along into the higher level "vertical integration." In other words, you integrate or combine the lower into the higher.

Thus to be able to reason at Level II does not mean that a person no longer is able to reason in the self-interests of Level I, but rather that he has become able to reason with Level II characteristics and is predominantly inclined to reason at this higher level.

Consider the implications of vertical integration: even after developing into a Level III capability and typically making moral decisions on a highly principled basis, the person is still capable of reverting all the way to Level I reasoning if the conditions of duress or threat are sufficiently strong.

Thus it is best not to think of ourselves or others as being *at* or being *in* a given level of moral reasoning. It is more correct to say that we are *capable of* or *inclined toward* reasoning at a certain level.

The great value of educational experiences is not that they change a person's structure, but that they help him explore and use the implications of the moral reasoning of which he is capable. Remember that the development process is "built in" and can be relied upon to emerge if the individual is engaged in experiences that require moral choices and also if he is being encouraged to reflect on the meaning and value of these choices.

FAMILY MODELING

It is important to provide consistent models for children. Yet parents soon realize that consistency is hard. If all of our moral influences were limited by the examples we set, we would likely fail in good parenting. But children can grow up to be even more moral than their parents. They are capable of growing beyond the models they encounter in parents and teachers. They can continue to develop a higher structure of moral judgment if the opportunity for dialogue and social interaction is available. As far as the family is concerned, what is most important in terms of this opportunity? Being on good terms with every family member!

It is never too early to engage a child in simple reasoning about right and wrong. The reasoning may not have much effect in Level I and not much more in Level II, but you can't wait until Level III arrives to start. The relationship between the parent and the child has to contain the fundamental respect and acceptance that will provide a basis for mature dialogue and transaction.

Many parents ask for help in building a relationship with a child in trouble. The rapport that is so hard to achieve in bad times should have been established in good times—but it didn't seem needed then; the child was so obedient and responsive.

The family should be a just and moral community. Family members are more important than the house or the furnishings or wealth. All members need mutual respect and a shared concern for righteousness. To maintain the proper moral tone, there must be a continuing concern for the quality of justice in the family. Each member participates in the quest. Try these suggestions in your family to promote the proper moral climate:

● Discuss moral matters in order to increase awareness of life's moral and ethical decisions.

• Participate in the improvement of justice in the home and family. To do this, each person needs a sense of involvement in the family's decision-making.

• Read together and discuss the Bible and Bible stories to become familiar with authoritative moral and spiritual teachings.

• Talk over your personal experiences and development, with special emphasis on matters of *why*.

Chapter 10

WHAT DOES GOD WANT?

Part of being human is learning to accept the complexities of life and to set priorities. From among the things that God values and wants us to value, this chapter suggests four things that God wants of us: that we accept responsibility, love Him, obey Him, and have faith in Him. In terms of your awareness of your own life, which of these need more attention?

PEOPLE WHO ARE RESPONSIBLE

God made us able to make moral choices. Each person's moral choices are influenced by many factors. But when a choice is made, the person who made the choice is responsible.

Responsibility is a value among God's people, but lately it has been popular to evade moral responsibility in a great game of passing the buck. We have come to recognize how important environment and influences from other people can be. We see that what we do is determined mainly by what we have already experienced and learned. Thus it becomes easy to push this awareness into an argument that no one should be held responsible for anything he says or does.

People laughed about this tendency in the 1950s when *West Side Story's* Officer Krupke was told that juvenile delinquents' problems should be blamed on society. It is no longer a laughing matter, because this argument has become the basis of defense for murder in Florida and rape in California. Defense attorneys have tried to put the blame on television. The defendants killed because they had seen so much killing that they no longer considered it wrong. Thus, the key legal element for a criminal act—ability to discriminate between right and wrong—was missing.

Such a view of moral responsibility has one major flaw. It assumes that the human being has a moral conscience as blank as a new cassette tape. The experiences of life make impressions on this tape, and whatever one does with the resulting sense of right and wrong is no more than a playback of the tape. Such a view leaves us no way to determine anyone's responsibility. Yet God has created in us not only the ability to make moral decisions but also a basic sense to distinguish between good and evil.

PEOPLE WHO LOVE GOD

God wants people to love Him. More precisely, God wants people to *choose* to love Him. Ever since the Garden of Eden, God has been restoring His relationship with human beings. God, the just and righteous Creator of the universe, has also been active as the Redeemer. Redeeming or buying back humankind is necessary because of sin. God's righteousness hates sin; God's justice requires punishment for sin. But God's love provides a way for people, no matter how sinful, to find fellowship with Himself. "For God so loved the world that He gave His one and only Son, that whoever believes in Him shall not perish but have eternal life" (John 3:16).

Two doctrines, God as Creator and God as Redeemer, are

the foundations of Christian faith. All that we are and all that we value as good are based on these two beliefs. Thus we value beauty because God created it. We value nature because God created it. We value truth because in what He made and what He has said in His Word, God is Truth. He gives us truthful pictures of reality. He does not mislead or confuse us. We value people and our relationships with people because God made them, and no matter how distorted by sin a person may be, God still loves him or her and so should we.

Indeed, love is at the center of these values—a special kind of love, not the trite and selfish love so popular in the world today. The Bible says there are two ways we know we are in God's love: we keep God's commandments (1 John 5:2) and we love one another (1 John 4:21).

PEOPLE WHO OBEY GOD

Obedience to God's Word and to God's will is very important. The Christian knows that a life of morality depends on obedience. Since what is moral is defined by the principles of God's Law, obedience to God's Law (or to the principles of the Law) is the way of morality and moral life. When Jesus said, "I am the way" (John 14:6), He was referring, in part, to the life of obedience.

Beyond the matter of living a moral life, the Christian knows that happiness and success are also dependent on obedience. For the Christian, life's purpose is defined and determined in terms of glorifying God. Whatever glorifies God and honors Him carries with it the by-product of personal success and fulfillment. Unlike the secular person, the Christian should not value material success and power as primary goals.

Indeed, we suspect that even for secular people, success and power are goals that are always beyond reach. The closer one gets, the further away the goal seems. If wealth is the measure of success, it always takes a little bit more to be really successful. If power and authority are measures of success, one never has enough.

Happiness as a goal is even more difficult to achieve. What produces happiness is less a matter of "big" things than of the little sparkling jewels of moment-by-moment experiences. I have seen people at their "finest hour," receiving high honors in recognition for great achievements, turning from the applause to their persistent sadness.

I know a professor who is recognized worldwide. He was honored in Stockholm for his research on heredity. But he would have traded it all for a second chance with his wife and children. When he lost them, he suddenly woke up to the tragedy that his neglect had created. The high points of life are few and far between for those whose values are locked into themselves. Their sadness runs deep.

On the other hand, I have been among people who end each day in bone-tired weariness, those for whom life seems to hold no recognition and little material reward. Some of these "little" people of God's kingdom have an abiding peace and sense of worth. Their actions and their contributions are known best to God. His approval is reward enough.

Christians are sometimes accused of being "otherworldly." Are we really so preoccupied with life hereafter that we can't keep our minds on things here? Indeed, some Christians use their eternal security as an emotional escape. Others see everything in terms of eternity and thus they fail to take their present responsibilities seriously. That's not what God intended.

The Christian has a blessed hope that gives life greater meaning. Beyond this life there is an eternal fellowship with the saints of all time in the presence of our Lord Jesus Christ. This reality is a great underlining of the value of obedience. We obey Christ because we are involved with Him in an eternal fellowship.

Obedience is at the heart of our relationship with God. Happiness and success are values that make no sense to the Christian apart from God's will. This may sound as if Christianity were locked into Level II moral judgment—response to moral authority from outside in the form of examples, rules, and regulations. Indeed, Kohlberg and others have seen Christianity just this way.

But Kohlberg pointed out that the basic values of life are seen differently at each level. In Level I, obedience is a matter of avoiding punishment and striving for reward. Goodness, in this view of obedience, is conforming to whatever demands have clout. Obedience, in Level I terms, has the tone of *forced* obedience.

In Level II, obedience means recognizing and willingly putting oneself under subjection to external authority. Examples, rules, and laws are accepted as the basis for an orderly moral life. Those who study such things see religion, in general, working this way. A person who becomes more religious also becomes more obedient to the examples, rules, and laws of the particular religious teaching.

Jesus said, "You have heard that it was said to the people long ago, 'Do not murder, and anyone who murders will be subject to judgment.' But I tell you that anyone who is angry with his brother will be subject to judgment" (Matthew 5:21-22). The Bible emphasizes not rules but principles. If you really understand what God wants, you know that it is not simply obedience to God's Law as to rules, but obedience to God's Law as to principles like mercy, compassion, love— concern for people! (Note the basis for this statement in Matthew 9:13 and 12:7.)

In Level III obedience is not forced (as in Level I) or merely willing (as in Level II), so much as it is natural. Obedience in Level III comes out of a relationship. It is a response of a loving involvement, a deep fellowship—oneness.

"Your wish is my command." Only to a person whose trust you share deeply can you say this and really mean it. When two people grow together, they make their decisions more and more together. So it is with our relationship with Jesus Christ. Obedience becomes an essential part of the relationship we have with Him.

Christ is our Master. In Level I, this matter of being a servant of God likely has an element of fear and forced service about it. In Level II it has an element of compliance and legalism about it. But the great revelation that comes with moral maturity into Level III is that our experience as God's servant changes our perspective. No longer is it a matter that we *must* serve God or even that we *ought* to serve God, but that it is *natural* that we serve God—we have a new nature. By faith we walk with God.

God is transforming us, bringing into us the mind of Christ—who, knowing full well that He was in power and authority, put all of it aside in order to become a servant, fulfilling God's will even to the sacrifice of His life; after this, God highly exalted Him (Philippians 2:5-11). God wants us to value obedience as Jesus did. Not because we must be obedient or that we ought to be obedient, but that in being transformed, we *are* obedient to God.

In the transformed life of mature Christian experience, obedience is hand in hand with trust. As we learn to trust God, obedience becomes firm. The emergence of obedience and trust says much about the quality of faith. Following is a chart in which the relationship is suggested.

PEOPLE WHO TRUST GOD

"Do not worry about tomorrow" (Matthew 6:34). Amazing, isn't it, that some Christians can be such anxious, uptight people. Jesus taught that His followers should live a day at a time, not fretting about what might happen. In fact, the teach-

THE DEVELOPMENT OF
OBEDIENCE, TRUST, AND FAITH

LEVELS OF MORAL JUDGMENT	OBEDIENCE	TRUST	FAITH
LEVEL I	Obedience emerges	—	Confidence in consequences
LEVEL II	Obedience is firm	Trust emerges	Belief in God's Law as rules for behavior
LEVEL III	Obedience is natural	Trust is firm	Faith in God's Law as principles for personal relationship (with God and with others)

ing of Jesus in Luke 12:22-34 sounds like a good excuse for not doing much planning. But rare is the Christian who doesn't get anxious from time to time.

In some ways it is easier for a non-Christian to be relaxed about important matters. When basic values are involved, the Christian is more apt to see the life-changing possibilities and to be concerned about them. For example, whether a young person takes God into account in making some of life's major decisions is of great concern to Christian parents. The education or vocational training a person chooses will increase or decrease his or her sensitivity to God's calling for life vocation.

Decisions about marriage—whether to get married, to

whom, why, and when—have profound effects on the quality of life and the spiritual welfare of the person. How one uses time, from late childhood on, has a great influence on the contribution he or she will make to others and on the worth of life itself.

Since the Christian assumes that life has purpose and that certain outcomes of life are more valuable than others, all of these decisions are important. They may be important to some non-Christians, as well, but the Christian is far more apt to see beyond the immediate outcomes, especially to see beyond short-term happiness and to be concerned in a deeply serious way.

Is it right for Christians to be so intense and so serious? Does that reflect the depth of faith Jesus teaches us to have? Once again, a specific teaching of the Bible seems to be somewhat inconsistent with the realities of a godly life. We must keep things in perspective.

The idea "don't be concerned about tomorrow" is not an absolute so much as a comparison. Compared with the planning that a person without faith must do (or at least *should* do) if he or she is even half aware of the hazards that lie around the corner, the Christian's approach to preparing and planning is a combination of faith and action. The difference is the *faith* factor.

Because a child of God has faith, tomorrow's burdens can wait until tomorrow. A Christian rarely has any good reason to lose sleep fretting. God will provide. "My grace is sufficient for you" (2 Corinthians 12:9). For Christians, planning is a matter of doing today what God sets before us. In faith, we know that today *is* the preparation for tomorrow.

When a burden of unfinished work or a sense of unpreparedness keeps me from sleep, I see it as a kind reminder and an invitation from God. Almost always, such fretful nights come after a time when I have been making careless choices.

My priorities have become sloppy. Instead of using my time and energy to do only the most important things, I have been trying to do everything all at once. So when I try to sleep, God keeps me awake—kindly reminding me to get back into the *valuing* business. I must take responsibility for making my own choices. God wants me to get my moral self back into action—to think through the unfinished work and the demands of tomorrow and decide what is most important. It can't possibly be everything.

When my life gets so jammed up with fretting that I can't even sleep, I get up and make a list of the things that I am concerned about. Then I write down practical steps that I could take to deal with each *important* problem. It takes time, but it feels better than tossing and turning in bed.

Making the list is the first step. Next, I prayerfully think about the importance of each item. I ask God to help me see the really important matters and set my priorities. It isn't numbness or less concern that I need; it is perspective.

When I've arranged my priorities, I copy the list again and put the important items at the top. What works for me might or might not be useful to you. Nevertheless, I can testify with confidence that God has never delayed in answering my prayers for a restored sense of values.

Sleeplessness or other signals that something is wrong could be God's way of giving you a kind reminder and a gentle invitation. The *reminder:* Life is better when you keep first things first. Decisions about priorities are at the heart of being fully human. The *invitation:* No matter how hopeless the pile of responsibilities and unfinished work may appear, getting things back to a healthy condition begins with making choices on the basis of values. Make your list. Prayerfully find the most important matters, and take at least one practical step toward the one or two that are most important.

We need not fret over tomorrow; we can live today with

God's priorities and know we will be adequate for tomorrow. God wants us to be responsible, yet not anxious or pushy. God wants us to love Him because we choose to. God wants us to obey Him because of our fellowship with Him. God wants us to have faith in Him—a faith that deepens because of trust and obedience.

FROM MORAL JUDGMENT TO MORAL ACTION

The connection between moral truth and moral action is easily broken. A person can know the right thing to do and not do it. A person can even want to do the right thing and fail to follow through.

Many critics of the moral judgment research point out that not enough attention is given to the matter of moral action. Indeed, every thoughtful Christian can agree that moral judgment alone is not sufficient. Other critics point out—correctly—that moral judgment, in the sense of rationalized mental processes that weigh out systematically every matter of right and wrong, is a very narrow view of what is involved. Emotions and habits are involved, and erratic unpredictability fits somewhere within the linkage between knowing to do the right and doing it.

God is not concerned primarily about moral judgment. He is concerned about behavior—about moral action. It is not enough to think righteous thoughts. The Bible teaches that the important outcome of learning is the practical use of what is learned. Scripture defines learning in terms of "obedience." To be obedient to God is to have learned the ways of godliness so thoroughly as to allow them to direct one's steps. But it is also more than that, since it is not within the power of any person to behave completely consistently with one's best intentions.

God must provide the *knowledge* on which truth-based moral decisions can be made; He must provide, through the transforming of the spirit, a *will* to please God in righteous behavior, and He must provide the *strength of character*, through the Holy Spirit living within the person, that will provide the power to act upon one's rightly chosen and rightly intended moral decisions.

The Apostle Paul uses this three-element bridge between moral truth and moral action: "For what I do is not the good I want to do; no, the evil I do not want to do—this I keep on doing. Now if I do what I do not want to do, it is no longer I who do it, but it is sin living in me that does it" (Romans 7:19-20). All three elements are represented here: the knowledge of good, the will to do good, and the capability to act upon the informed will. In Paul's illustration it is this last element that is not in place.

If a godly person such as Paul found that knowing and willing to do righteously were not enough, then the issue of strength to follow through on informed good intentions is serious indeed.

The diagram following suggests a relationship among all three of these necessary components. If any one piece of the bridge should be missing, the result will be a gap between moral truth and moral action.

The message of James, with its emphasis on putting faith into action—action that will illustrate the faith—is also consistent with this view. What God wants is a moral person—a person who fulfills in action what the Word teaches about godly living. Through one's own efforts no one even comes close to being a perfect fulfillment of what God wants. But in the walk of faith the Christian benefits from God's renewal process as begun at conversion. Thus the Christian grows in acceptance of responsibility toward God and toward fulfilling God's work in human society. At the center of godly living is love for God, obedience to his teachings, and continuously reaffirmed faith in Jesus Christ as Lord.

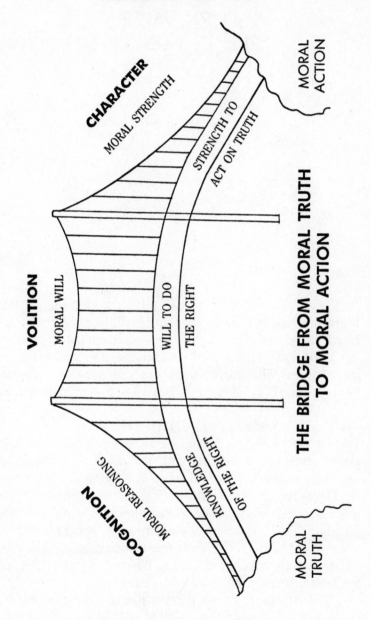

THE BRIDGE FROM MORAL TRUTH
TO MORAL ACTION

Chapter 11

WHEN VALUES
ARE IN CONFLICT

All sorts of trivial matters lead to clashes, but in this chapter we will focus on conflicts of moral values. What values are important enough to concern us? What can parents do to encourage the development of these values? What can be done when we see another person "going wrong"? What are the dangers of a conflict in values?

THE FREEDOM TO CHOOSE

Putting up protective barriers around small children helps keep them from wandering into the street. But fences are useful for only a few years. Parents can't keep children inside the fences forever. The human being develops through exploring. Moral values are not developed through meaningless rituals and habits. They are developed through thoughtful choices about moral matters. If there is freedom to choose, there must be freedom to make a bad choice. Where there is no freedom to choose, there is no freedom to learn.

God has made us to possess moral judgment. He has enabled us to deal with the reality of evil. Where did evil come from? Why did God allow the presence of evil in the Garden of Eden? It had to be. Could Adam and Eve really share in or even recognize God's moral character without facing moral choices themselves? God created in humans a capacity to share in God's own appreciation of righteousness.

Genesis 3 shows us that Eve was impressionable. Perhaps she was even a bit gullible. No matter how much she may have wanted to believe God and to please Him, she tended to doubt Him. She was willing to take a chance on a different moral choice.

Adam showed these same traits, yet he went one step further. When confronted by his error, he tried to shift the responsibility. Sin makes us quick to transfer our moral responsibilities. That way we don't have to face up to sin as a reality. The Apostle James wrote that we are tempted to sin when we are "dragged away" by our own evil desires (James 1:14).

The Genesis account begins the long saga of God's actions to bring sinful humankind back into fellowship with Himself. God provided a solution for sin. The short-term solution was in animal sacrifices. These sacrifices provided a basis of obedience and symbolized that people are at God's mercy because of sin. The long-term solution became clear when Jesus Christ fulfilled the conditions of the death penalty on behalf of all who believe.

The Christian's moral righteousness does not depend on doing good works in order to earn merit and favor with God. Instead, our relationship to God depends on Christ's righteousness. "God made Him [Christ] who had no sin to be sin for us, so that in Him we might become the righteousness of God" (2 Corinthians 5:21).

God accepts the Christian as being without sin. Since the penalty for sin has been paid by Jesus Christ, the guilt of sin has been removed "as far as the east is from the west" for those who belong to Christ. God knows that His children continue to sin. For this He makes provision. He accepts us in a process of continuing forgiveness, not because of our good intentions, but because of Christ.

Through Christ we enter into a special relationship with God called a *new birth* and also called *adoption*. The biblical use of *adoption* always refers to rights and privileges, exactly as we use the word today. Being adopted brings a person formally and officially into a family; thus it involves a new identity. Becoming part of God's family brings about a change in values. For some, the evidence of this value change is soon in coming. In others, it is a slow process, so slow that onlookers may become skeptical.

God's influence and presence in the life of the Christian, also called the indwelling of the Holy Spirit, helps tip the moral balance toward God. Seldom does the Holy Spirit bring about instant moral reform. But just as the first Adam tended to make moral choices *away* from God, the Christian shares in the nature of God's "second Adam," Jesus Christ, and tends to choose *toward* God's values in moral matters.

God leaves all people free to choose. Those who reject are free to accept the consequences of rejection. God does not override their decisions or force them into a relationship with Himself. Those who do accept are free to develop slowly or more quickly, depending on their daily choices about walking close to God, being fed by His Word, and fellowshiping with others of His people. God does not demand a particular rate of spiritual growth.

GOD AS FATHER

The Bible uses the word *Father* in many places to describe God's relationships with His people. Sometimes, parents get carried away with this imagery and posture themselves as God-on-earth for their children. This can be dangerous and can give children a very faulty view of God.

God is Creator, Provider, Judge, and Redeemer. When a human being attempts to "play God," this overstepping results in disaster, for the parent also must accept God as Father. Parents are God's servants, ministering to the child as provider and teacher. The Bible gives us all of these aspects of God. But when it deals with God in very personal terms, the Bible uses the word *Father*. In these passages, God is the gentle and just Provider—concerned, protecting, and reliable.

Insofar as the parent represents God, especially in the life of a little child, this representation should show God's gentleness, His patience, His continuing nurture and care. The Holy Scripture faithfully represents Him this way. His is not the vindictive and harshly judgmental parenting that some Christians act out!

God liberates His children, making us free to be real people, free to develop, to explore, to find ourselves, and to find His purposes for our lives. Should Christian parents do otherwise? Don't be offended when a young man or woman pleads, "Don't fence me in!" Sometimes it is hard for parents to accept this need for freedom, because they have dreams for their children. Wise parents must take care not to manipulate their children into fulfilling their own dreams.

Compulsive parenting is dangerous. Children should not be driven. The Bible warns that fathers are to see that their children obey "with proper respect" (1 Timothy 3:4). The parent's dignity and the child's dignity are both involved. God's Law is concerned with respect and love as defined by righteousness: "Fathers, do not embitter your children, or they will become discouraged" (Colossians 3:21).

People who have had all the advantages of a Christian home and family sometimes go wrong. The biblical promise (Proverbs 22:6) that when the child is old he or she will not "depart from the way" is hard to square with appearances.

What does it mean to "train a child in the way he should go"? Does *train* mean to create in the child a set of mechanical habits? Indeed not. God's nature and His values point to an entirely different meaning of *training*.

Since God has created us as creatures of will and moral choice, He respects our freedom to choose—even if we choose not to believe in His Son. God punishes for the wrong choices, but the freedom to persist in wrong choices is there. God does not make decisions *for* people. Nor does God force all persons to conform to His will.

Christian parents are not to treat their children as horses or dogs, training them to jump through moral and ethical hoops. Notice who responds to the applause after the trained animal act—the trainer! Bringing up children is sometimes similar. Parents who seek applause for their spirituality train their children to do all the right things at the right times— even if they have to violate the integrity of the children in order to "train the act." Training children as if they were animals is an old and misguided human tendency that was given a substantial boost around mid-century by the behaviorists, especially by B.F. Skinner. God does not ask for an animal show. Instead, He demands a continuous process that consists of far more than rewards and punishment. The process includes setting examples—reliable, continuous examples. It involves setting rules and establishing responsibility. Most important, it requires a long-term dialogue focused on the motives behind the behavior.

TRUSTING GOD'S GOODNESS

Learning to trust God's basic goodness is one evidence of spiritual maturity. Trust finds one of its most basic fulfillments in prayer. A direct expression of spirituality, prayer is the most intimate experience associated with development of the spiritual center-point of a person's life. Through prayer one gives tangible expression to the relationship of trust in God.

Hand in hand with trust is the self-respect that seeks answers. "Why, God? Please show me Your purposes." God has purposes; life is not some wild, unpredictable nightmare. But in order that our trust might grow, sometimes the answers to our questions come very slowly. This was Job's experience.

In the oldest book of the Bible, God deals with values. Job had all the good things of life. He was a rich man by secular standards (a fine house, land, power, wealth) as well as by standards a Christian can respect: family, self-respect, love. Job was a man of honorable values.

But God's plan for Job was to bring him to a deeper sense of spiritual trust. Job lost everything that seemed important except his relationship to God. Crushed down by physical and emotional suffering, he was indeed a man to be pitied.

His friends weren't much help. They decided that Job was being punished for something he must have done to offend God. Even his wife, rejecting him, looked for an easy answer. "Look how God is treating you, and for no good reason! Death itself would be an improvement over your terrible suffering. Curse God and die!" (Job 2) But Job did not. He was a godly man throughout the ordeal.

Instead of cursing God, he came face-to-face with Him in a deeper sense of trust. Job saw that in God and in His righteousness are the ultimate values of life (Job 42:1-6). Afterward, he was healed by God and returned to a life of even greater happiness, wealth, and honor. Again, the good things of life that God gave him seemed to vindicate Job as a righteous man.

Is this a story of how the good guys always win in the end? Indeed, no. Job's story reaches its climax at the point when he learned how basic and how adequate is trust in God. His faith became the high point of triumph even though Job was a penniless, sick, and pitiable man. His triumph was in his trust in God, not in the rewards that followed. Indeed, the good things of life don't always follow. Many are the saints of God whose only visible reward will be in heaven.

Parents can trust God's goodness for themselves and their children, thus avoiding the terrible mistake of assuming too much responsibility for what their children become. God asks nothing beyond our willingness to cooperate in His work in people's lives. He does not hold us responsible for what others choose to do with their lives. In love we should show our concern, but we only hurt ourselves by feeling guilty.

Take courage from the story Jesus told of a grown son who chose against his father and against God. He asked for his share of the family inheritance. Apparently, he was old enough to be eligible, yet what an insult to the rest of the family. The father went along with his son's wishes.

As the story unfolds (Luke 15:11-32), it is clear that the father felt that his son was completely lost—virtually dead, at least spiritually. We see only a little of the father's grief. Instead the story is focused on the young man's experiences and his view of himself. As he hit bottom, he reflected on what he had lost. Then he repented and returned. The father had not searched for him. No pleading letters had been written. The son was in God's hands all along.

The father's hurt was deep, the longing great. He watched the roadway. One day he spotted his son in the distance. "He's coming back! Thank God!"

Every story does not end like this, but God is in control. God loves His children. One of the greatest reassurances we have is that God does not want any to perish but for all to come to repentance (2 Peter 3:9).

GUIDING MORAL DEVELOPMENT

What can parents do? Indeed, what can any of us do for each other that will be helpful in dealing with the conflicts that emerge as we develop? Here are seven tasks that can and should be undertaken to guide moral development.

• Stimulate inquiry. Moral conflicts cannot be resolved apart from understanding. What is the issue? What is at stake? What are the consequences? We need to stimulate each other's inquiry into these questions. Moral development absolutely depends on it.

• Stimulate verbalization. Not everyone finds it easy to talk about important things. It's easier to talk about baseball and the weather. But we need to help each other find ways to talk about the moral conflicts we face. This may mean enlarging the vocabulary, especially in dealing with children. Without the use of language to share and to discuss, moral development is slowed severely.

• Ask "Why?" Children should try to find their own answers to this question. Moral conflicts and moral development respond to the deeper look at *why*. "Never mind that we disagree," you might say, "just tell me why you see it that way." Seeking understanding comes first; seeking agreement should *follow*.

• Provide experiences in which issues are examined. People who are developing together, as in a family, need common experiences. In order to talk about moral aspects of life, you need to share similar experiences. Acts of kindness shared together such as visiting the sick or bereaved, taking flowers to a neighbor, or working together make sense even to small children *if* they are discussed and the moral issues made clear. Experience and discussion of the good side of life provide the skills needed when the rough spots of conflict must be resolved.

• Dialogue (listen responsively). Moral conflicts respond best to honest dialogue. Conflicts are rarely resolved by speech-making. Even if only one person is wrong, the process of communication demands that all involved have a chance to be heard. We all need to develop the skill of listening responsively. The secret is to *listen* instead of planning your reply. When you do say something, make sure you're responding to what the other person has said.

● Explore disequilibrium. Disequilibrium means realizing that your basic beliefs seem inadequate. It occurs at several points in normal moral development. It sounds like this: "Dad, I've always believed that God made the world and that He is interested in me, but I'm really wondering now." The temptation is to hide such heresy under the rug. "But, Bill, you can't possibly mean that." Stop! Try this instead: "You've got some things to think through. Let's talk. Why don't you tell me how you're looking at it now?" Exploring *with* the person is far more helpful than trying to provide immediate "corrections."

● Stand alongside. When all is said and done, it's being there that counts the most. The Holy Spirit stands alongside as the presence of God with us. Even so, the major contribution we can make to others, especially within the family, is to stand alongside—especially in times of conflict.

Chapter 12

THE CONFLICTS AHEAD

Religious freedom runs deep in our historical tradition. For many early colonists who came to North America from Europe, freedom to worship God in their own way was extremely important. Even while America was still a group of British colonies, the reputation of this continent was established. Here was a safe haven for persecuted Christians.

CHRISTIAN NATIONS?

The United States and Canada have been called Christian nations mainly because of their tendency to consider Christian values. In their governments and in their homes, the people of these nations have been seen as basically Christian.

Historians don't all agree that calling either the United States or Canada a Christian nation is accurate, but the tradition is there. Freedom to worship God has been a cornerstone in their development.

One unfortunate by-product of living in a "Christian" nation is that we tend to take religion for granted. We become flabby Christians. Just as one's body needs exercise, one's religious beliefs need to be put to work—and the tougher the going, the stronger we become.

Consider what it has meant to be a Christian in China since 1945. For many years the only stories we heard from behind the Bamboo Curtain concerned hardship and persecution of Christians. To those of us in the Western nations it sounded as if the church, planted by over a century of missionary effort, was being systematically annihilated. How could any group stand up to such overwhelming opposition and cruelty?

Then China began to open up in Mao's last several years. At first the story seemed too good to believe: millions and millions of Christians and a variety of churches, large and small, some still meeting secretly and others feeling that the time had come for more open worship in the name of Jesus Christ. Contrary to the expectations in the Western world, communism had not been able to conquer Christianity. In fact, it would be fair to say that it stimulated the church in China to grow at a phenomenal rate. Ease and softness are more threatening to the church than persecution, dictatorship, and communism.

Flabbiness and sloppiness are not pleasing to God. He did not intend for us to sit and watch life go by. Jesus said to His disciples, "You are the salt of the earth. But if the salt loses its saltiness, how can it be made salty again? It is no longer good for anything" (Matthew 5:13).

Christians are to stand for something. God's attitude toward no-account Christianity is also revealed in these words to the church at Laodicea, "I know your deeds, that you are neither cold nor hot. . . . So, because you are lukewarm, neither hot nor cold—I am about to spit you out of My mouth" (Revelation 3:15-16).

Where Christians don't really stand for anything and where there are few pressures on the church, a soft and mushy

Christian experience results. Then God allows persecution to move in. At times like these throughout history, the church has toughened up and stood for something. The text in Revelation about the church at Laodicea illustrates this idea: "Those whom I love I rebuke and discipline. So be earnest, and repent. . . . To him who overcomes, I will give the right to sit with Me on My throne" (Revelation 3:19-21).

Conflict is necessary to strengthen the church in the world. The great moments of forward movement of the church have often followed after persecution. Such a period may be about to break in upon *us*.

The Christian view of family values is close to the top of the list of issues likely to cause friction in the near future. I have three reasons for believing this. First, in the Christian community the family cannot be abandoned; it is basic. Second, the Christian family is now well on the way to being distinctly different from the secular family (or whatever substitute for the family secular society may create). Finally, the pressure of secular society on this increasingly different family—the Christian family—can have certain strengthening outcomes for the church.

For several years, the television schedule has been full of programs that scoff at family values; now there has been a turn-around, at least in part. Amidst the hundreds of programs that show fatherless families and casual live-in partnerships, there are several very successful and long-running serial programs that portray balanced and reasonably sane homes where parents show love and concern and children show respect. What a relief! Christians should show producers and sponsors their approval in substantial ways.

Nevertheless, the positive signs we see are still vastly outnumbered. A values battle will continue to rage in this society and around the world in matters of family. Christians need to stand up for biblical standards.

SECULARISM

Secularism describes the human condition apart from God. When we refer to the secular society, we mean the non-Christian majority of mankind, including the institutions, customs, and standards by which people live in ignorance or rejection of God. Notice how secularism has already invaded the Christian community.

Crucial secular values of our times are *self-centeredness*, *materialism*, and *humanism*. These three values could be stretched into dozens of points, described in altogether different terms, or even reduced to one item—sinfulness.

● Adults who have been stunted in their moral judgment still think of moral choices as children do in self-centered terms. Self-centeredness is not a choice for such persons; it is the trap in which they are caught. Moral immaturity is a consequence of sin. Such people see everything as either good or bad, right or wrong, evil or righteous according to how it works out for them.

● Materialism is evident in the lawful but unprincipled choices people make apart from God. If one does not see God as the basis of rules and standards, then two problems occur. First, the standards of society have no clear basis and must be constantly challenged and frequently changed. Second, the standards and rules of society are relative to each situation that comes up. What is right today may be wrong tomorrow.

In this chaos, each person reaches out for something to hold. Since moral standards are not seen as reliable, even human relationships are not trustworthy. What else is there in which to put one's confidence? Things. Preoccupation with possessions and the tendency to treat people as objects are characteristic of many people who reason at Level II of moral judgment.

Some materialism is better explained as evidence of self-ishness or self-centeredness, and thus it should be seen as

Level I judgment. But to suggest that all of the materialism in our society is a matter of selfishness is too simple. Consider the many people who amass great wealth with the intention of using it to help others. How easy it is for them to fall into the materialistic error of valuing properties and monuments more than relationships with people.

When people are limited in their moral judgment to the structure of Level II, they easily fall prey to the materialism that is motivated by human competition. Even in doing humanitarian good works, being preoccupied with what others will value tends toward materialistic activity. (We should not forget that Christians are often caught in these same secular tendencies because of the powerful influences of our society.)

● A principled sort of humanism is the secular form of Level III moral judgment. People without God must base their principles on humanity itself. Truth as a principle is valuable because it is part of the humanistic basis for social trust. Love as a principle is valuable because it gives quality to the social experience. For the humanist, the ultimate principle is life itself. Thus, such a person brings all matters of right and wrong to center around the principle of life. Some have called it reverence for life.

The great secular philosophers have wrestled with the principles of life, trying to find its meaning. For better or worse, the value of life itself seems to be the dead end of humanism; in the words of a dismal secular song, "Is that all there is?" Without hope of life beyond the grave, much of the value of mortal life never comes clear. Humanism as a moral philosophy provides very few answers to the *whys* of life.

BIBLICAL RESPONSES

To respond to these three secular values, we need to think in biblical terms. Never forget that these issues impact the church and the Christian family too. They aren't just outsiders' problems; they are ours.

• Level I. "Do to others as you would have them do to you" (Luke 6:31). The biblical answer for self-centeredness is very direct. Treat others as you want them to treat you. This is practical advice, though it is very difficult for a person who is self-centered. Such a person can tell you what should be done to please himself or herself. "What's in it for me?" is the basic language of self-centeredness. Jesus wisely accepts this starting place and switches the moral obligation so that it works both ways: to *others* as to *you*.

Scholars in the field of moral development point out that this so-called Golden Rule is heavy teaching to expect a child to understand. Indeed, a young child would lack the sense of what it is like to be someone else. Thus, although it is memorized by many youngsters, the full meaning may not come to light until they are between the ages of eight and eleven.

Jesus first gave the Golden Rule to adults who were secularized by the basic human tendency to be self-centered. This inclination to think first of themselves was working against their moral development. They were still morally underdeveloped children.

Does this problem exist today? Indeed, yes. Our society is weakened by a self-centeredness that asks, "What's in it for me?" Being concerned about others is out of style for some people. "If it feels good, do it" and "Look out for number one" are the slogans of many in our secular society. It even gets into the Christian family and into the church in the form of individualism and selfish egoism. Whenever we put our own concerns and interests ahead of our concern for others, our Lord is not pleased.

• Level II. "Do not store up for yourselves treasures on earth" (Matthew 6:19). The biblical answer to materialism is very direct. No matter how satisfying, the piling up of wealth is not "where it's at" for Christians. There's nothing wrong with being responsible about providing for one's need and for one's family, but it easily gets out of hand.

A person who gains in material things becomes more concerned about order and protection. When our valuing of law and order is primarily in terms of protection for ourselves and our goods, something is wrong. If we follow Jesus' teaching about material wealth, law and order take on new meaning. We can focus attention on the protection of the rights and welfare of others.

• Level III. "I am the way and the truth and the life. No one comes to the Father except through Me" (John 14:6). One of the main concerns of humanism is truth because it is the cornerstone of science and the major emphasis of philosophy. What, then, is truth?

Jesus boldly answers, "I am the truth." Whatever science discovers is because of truth; Christ the cocreator put it there to be discovered. Whatever mankind creates in the arts, music, and literature is because of truth; Christ the cocreator put it within men and women to share the true creative arts. Whatever philosophers understand of the truth is possible because of the inherent trueness of God's universe. Thus, through human studies, creative acts, explorations, and experiments, men and women grope toward a grasp of truth. Jesus Christ steps from the fog-draped unknown and announces, "I am the way and the truth and the life."

Christians need not grope blindly for truth. Instead, as those who know the Person who is the originator and the source of whatever is discovered as truth, we can join as competent participants in truly humanistic activities and pursuits.

THE FALL OF TRADITION

At the practical level, much of the conflict we face in society comes from the fall of tradition. In recent years, drastic changes have taken place, most of which can be traced to technology. Their effects are worldwide. Although it is easier and more comfortable to live with the past, change cannot be turned back. As Tevye cried in *Fiddler on the Roof*, "Tradition! Tradition!" Where has tradition gone?

Dramatic changes in human thought and values have come about because of computers, automation, nuclear energy, the shrinking world of fast transportation and instant communication, increasing international conflict, terrorism, and the energy shortage. No wonder traditions are changing!

Traditions help to stabilize society. People need to be able to count on something. So when traditions fall, people are confused because they've lost their point of reference. The stress is greatest on the elderly.

Consider the matter of clothing. Arguments about the proper way to dress occur in many families so that decisions about how to dress appropriately for particular events have become a home battlefield. The conflicts and arguments are only symptoms. The basic issue has to do with traditional versus pragmatic valuing.

A pragmatic person or society decides whether or not something is worthwhile by asking, "Does it work?" or "What is it good for?" Pragmatism values things, ideas, and people not for their own worth but because of what they can *do*.

As our society becomes more pragmatic, it becomes less traditional. Those who hold traditional ways are often considered old-fashioned and in conflict with those who hold pragmatic ways.

In matters of proper dress, as in many other things, young people tend to make their decisions on the basis of what they believe others will do. "But, Dad, *nobody* wears a tie to church." Nobody? Nobody Bob thinks to be important. Indeed, conformity is a strong factor in most people's decisions about what to wear. As traditions fall, conformity remains. To what will the Christian be conformed?

There will be terrible times in the last days. People will be lovers of themselves, lovers of money, boastful, proud, abusive, disobedient to their parents, ungrateful, unholy, without love, unforgiving, slanderous, without self-control, brutal, not lovers of the good, treacherous, rash, conceited, lovers of pleasure rather than lovers of God— having a form of godliness but denying its power (2 Timothy 3:1-5).

These ungodly values can overtake Christians. If we seek "praise from men more than praise from God" (John 12:43), we will soon have no place to stand.

Chapter 13

THE GREATEST
OF VALUES

Christian values? One word says them all: *love*. The principle that holds together all of God's dealings with mankind, the principle that Jesus emphasized in what He called "a new commandment," the reason for the cross, is love.

Love of God for people, love of the redeemed for God the Saviour, and love of people for each other are the three basic kinds of love. The Bible reveals God acting toward people in love. Even when acting in judgment, God in love made a way of reconciliation for His own people. The Bible shows the fulfillment that comes to those who love God. The Bible also shows that love for others is the natural outgrowth of God's love for us.

But what is love? It is such an overworked word that we hear it thrown around in all sorts of loose ways. It slushes out of radios and stereos; it supposedly explains pathetic happenings in television dramas. It shows up in sentimental poems on February 14. Love is a word almost worn out from overuse—or maybe from misuse.

No matter where you slice into it, the Bible is full of love. It is the basis of God's message to mankind, for God loves and cares for people. The only danger is that *love* has been popularized into a romantic notion lacking in the tough-minded discipline of justice and selflessness necessary for godly love.

THE SOURCE

Where does love come from? Does it just spring up out of nowhere when our backs are turned? Hardly. Like most emotions, love is a response. We are most inclined to be loving when we are aware of being loved.

One of the most pleasant experiences in my life has been hiking in the mountains. It's especially great where the mountains are close enough together that hikers on one mountainside can see and hear hikers on the trail on the next mountain. Across the valley will come an echoing distant shout, "AahhLohhh." And you cup your hands beside your mouth and reply, "Hello!" Back and forth several times, no particular message, just the greeting of human beings letting each other in on the joy of life.

Love is that sort of experience. Love is back-and-forth sharing—often with no particular message—just letting another person in on your joy of living. But who starts the process? If love is a response, who makes the first move?

All love can be traced to one source. In creating mankind, God made Adam and Eve sharers of His own characteristics. Thus, the tendency to respond to love with love is a built-in trait. Those who seem to be without any trace of love in their lives usually have had little love shown them by other. But people who demonstrate a vast capability for loving are usually reflecting and responding to what they have known from others.

For the Christian, knowing God, the Source of love, should be enough to start the process, even if those nearby aren't showing much love. The Apostle John pulled it together in a very simple statement: "We love because He first loved us" (1 John 4:19).

However, Christians can make a mistake about love. We hear so much about it in sermons and Bible teaching that we must be careful not to think of love as a thing that we just *know* about.

"Jesus loves me, this I know."

Hold it! What do you mean, "Jesus loves me, this I *know*"? Try it this way: Jesus loves me, this I *feel!* Not very good poetry, but it adds the heart to the head. Love is not only a matter of knowing; it includes *feeling*, as well. It's reassuring to *know* that you are loved, but it's also important to *feel* loved.

But that heads us off in another dangerous direction. Love, real love, isn't just a warm puppy. It isn't just a fuzzy, floaty feeling. Love is solid, stubborn, and real. Its reality lies in the fact that it is both knowing and feeling. At the base of it, we know God, and thus we know His love. Through His Word, and through His creation, we know Him.

KINDS OF LOVE

What kinds of human love are there? Motherly love, brotherly love, marital love, patriotic love, and love for chocolate-covered doughnuts. There are different kinds of love and in some languages there are different words for each. The Greek language of Bible-times used different words for sensual love, family love, and godly love. Let's look at love through the three levels of moral judgment.

● Level I love. Self-centeredness shows up even in love. While the love is real enough, it doesn't have the other person at its center. Much sensual love is of this sort. "What can I get out of the relationship? What will I get in return for my acts of love? If I give, what will I get?"

For children, love of this sort can be expressed by exchanging gifts, by receiving and giving special attention at ceremonies such as birthday parties, Valentine's Day parties, and religious ceremonies of a concrete sort, such as Christmas programs and plays.

● Level II love. The rule-structured strength of Level II moral judgment puts some backbone in love. No longer flabby and self-centered, love is disciplined into a sense of duty and responsibility. While love sees from the loved one's viewpoint, it also has its do's and don'ts. There is a more orderly set of boundaries, a set of expectations for oneself and for others. Here we can say that love has its definition in a sense of justice and integrity.

Children learn to share in this sort of love as they develop responsibility and a sense of loyalty in the family. Their love for parents can be expressed in defensiveness and protective ways if other children or even adults criticize the child's parents. Sometimes, especially in well-knit families, a child will express love for a brother or sister this same way.

● Level III love. The highest form of love we can know is to live within the principle of love itself. Beyond all the sense of duty, beyond the concern for responsibilities and the mechanical aspects of give and take, love becomes a state of being. Love is the way we are. It shows through in the strength of personality that comes from inner peace. "The joy of the Lord is your strength" (Nehemiah 8:10). It affects all our relationships, especially those in the family.

It is hard to frustrate Level III love. It doesn't whine, "That's not fair!" It doesn't resent the moments of distance and frustration. It depends not on the qualifying terms of the relationship but on the relationship itself.

In Level III, love has become a state of inner peace that is expressed in the actions of life. The Bible refers to the peace that "transcends all understanding" (Philippians 4:7). Such love is not something you simply know about in your head; it is something that is deep in your whole being. Yes, you know it; yes, you feel it; but far more, you do not live in any aspect of life apart from it. Because of your love relationship, you have been transformed. You share yourself with others, and they become part of you. In His prayer for us, Jesus found these words to express this:

> My prayer is not for them alone. I pray also for those who will believe in Me through their message, that all of them may be one, Father, just as You are in Me and I am in You. May they also be in us. . . . I in them and You in Me. May they be brought to complete unity to let the world know that You sent Me and have loved them even as You have loved Me . . . that the love You have for Me may be in them and that I Myself may be in them (John 17:20-26).

ACTIVE LOVE

Love is not just a state of being. Love is something that you live out. Love is something that you *do*.

Jesus was trying hard to rebuild a relationship of trust with the Apostle Peter. Not many days before, Peter had abandoned Jesus when He most needed a friend. Peter had saved his own skin by swearing that he had never known Jesus. Making matters worse, he had broken his promise always to be faithful. He felt desperately guilty about it. So Jesus gave Peter a chance to renew their relationship of love (John 21:15-17).

"Do you love Me?" Jesus asked. "Yes, Lord, You know I do," Peter replied. What followed shows the sort of action that firms up love: "Take care of My sheep." Jesus asked Peter not only to say it, but to act on it. In this case, Peter's grief and guilt were so overwhelming that at first he was not able to claim the deep love that Jesus was talking about. Instead,

Peter used a simpler word for love. Never mind—Jesus seemed to say—make your love active, put it to work, and it will grow. "Feed My sheep."

SMOTHERING LOVE

A good gardener will warn, "Don't water it too much." In watering a plant, as in much of life, enough is enough; more is too much. How much love is too much?

If God's love is any example, there is no such thing as too much love. God's love is boundless. But we sometimes show love in unhealthy ways. Even the idea of good deeds can go sour. Once there was a cartoon showing a Boy Scout helping the legendary little old lady get across the street. But since in this case she didn't want to go across that particular street, she was kicking and screaming.

If we aren't alert to other people's needs and interests, we can impose loving acts upon them. Sometimes we smother them with loving acts of the wrong sorts.

The most dangerous of these is overprotection. Parents are particularly apt to run into this problem, but sometimes even husbands and wives do. It is indeed loving to have concern and even to be fearful for the welfare of a loved one at certain times. But there is no way that any of us can live another's life for him or her. We have to give people growing room and space to explore. Remember that where there is no chance to make a mistake, there is no chance to learn.

Oneness is a value of marriage, but the Christian model for oneness is the relationship of Christ and the church (the bride of Christ). Through the ages, Christ has been building His church, as He promised, but the church and Christ still have separate identities. Wives and husbands should develop their separate identities as well as a relational identity. Mothers and fathers should let children develop their own identities.

Even in the same family, children are not all so many peas in a pod. Each is a different person with a unique personality. No two of us are exactly alike. We are being conformed to the image of Christ (Romans 8:29), but we need to be careful not to expect another Christian, not even our children, to be conformed to *us*. The important conformity is to Christ, not just to some current notion of "good Christian behavior."

THE SIGN OF LOVE

People today like to wear signs. T-shirts and bumper stickers say a lot about what we are thinking and who we are. As people grow older, their signs become smaller, but they are still evident.

Consider the little cogwheel of the Rotary Club, the blue and gold "L" of the Lions Club, the two-eared jug of the Gideons. Oh, how nice it is to let people know who we are.

How do you let people know that you belong to Jesus Christ? Wear a little gold cross, of course. Will that do it? Perhaps it will offer a clue, but it is surely not good proof. The Bible says there is a sign of love among Christians, and it is not a gold cross on a chain or pin. "This is how we know who the children of God are and who the children of the devil are: Anyone who does not do what is right is not a child of God; nor is anyone who does not love his brother. This is the message you heard from the beginning: We should love one another" (1 John 3:10-11).

For the Christian, the sign of love is a two-part sign, even as the cross is a two-part emblem—a vertical beam and a horizontal beam. One part, the vertical, shows our love relationship with God. The horizontal part represents love for our brother. When the Apostle John used the word *brother*, it is likely that he meant our brothers and sisters in Christ and the extension of this love to all those who are "not yet Christians," as they say in Africa. Each of the two parts of the sign depends on the other part. The cross isn't a cross without both parts.

"This is how we know that we love the children of God: by loving God and carrying out His commands" (1 John 5:2).

"And He has given us this command: Whoever loves God must also love his brother" (1 John 4:21).

"If anyone says, 'I love God,' yet hates his brother, he is a liar" (1 John 4:20).

Jesus taught no restrictions on the objects of our love: "Love your enemies and pray for those who persecute you" (Matthew 5:44). "Do good to those who hate you, bless those who curse you, pray for those who mistreat you" (Luke 6:27-28).

The Apostle John reminds us that love starts at home. Our first concern is among those in the family. What sense does it make to show love outside if we can't be loving within the family? It may be easier to appear to be loving with someone we don't live with. The little things that rub us the wrong way are bearable and sometimes not even noticed in a series of short-term encounters. But those we are with day in and day out—that's another story. All the little flaws, habits, and mannerisms can irritate, unmercifully it seems. And that's where the principle of mature love comes in:

> Love is patient, love is kind,
> love is not jealous; love does not brag.
> It is not arrogant or rude.
> Love does not insist on its own way;
> it is not irritable or resentful;
> it does not rejoice at another being wronged—
> but rejoices in the right and with the truth.
> Love accepts all things, believes all things,
> hopes all things, endures all things.
> Love never ends
> (paraphrase of 1 Corinthians 13:4-8).

Practice these things at home, and they will become more natural among fellow Christians, at school, in the market, at work, and among those who need to know our Saviour.

SPIRITUAL DEVELOPMENT

Most of the ways in which human beings develop are observable. The tendency among people in a scientific society is to believe that only what is observable is real. Spirituality is not directly observable; therefore, things that are spiritual, and even the idea of the spiritual nature of the human being, are not taken very seriously.

The biblical authors were hard-pressed to give practical illustrations of the spiritual nature. The Apostle Paul, especially, wrote much about spirituality and the contrast between the carnal (fleshly or material) aspects and the spiritual center core of human reality. For his illustrations of the spiritual nature and its development, he most often drew his examples from the realm of physical development. It is clear that he saw parallels between the development that can be observed in the physical, mental, and emotional aspects of life and the development that cannot be observed in the spiritual center of human reality.

Of the aspects of development that can be observed, measured, and objectively described, the most obvious is physical development. Much of our understanding of spiritual development is based on understanding physical development. Three different New Testament authors—Paul, Peter, and the author of Hebrews—all dip into the same type of illustration to talk about how the spiritual center of the person gets "fed." The point to notice here is that the unseen nature of spiritual development, though mystical and accepted as reality by faith and not by sight, can be compared with an aspect of growth. Thus the Bible suggests that there are parallels between the spiritual nature and the observable aspects of human development. The references to *milk* as an appropriate nourishment for infants (1 Corinthians 3:2, Hebrews 5:12, and 1 Peter 2:2) encourage us to search for yet other ways in which spirituality—and especially spiritual *development*—may be parallel to other things we can know about human development by studying the observable aspects of personhood.

In addition to the physical aspects, we can learn more about intellectual or mental development, emotional development, social development, and moral development. Each tells *part* of the story of spiritual development. Each aspect is a linkage of the experiences of life with the vital center core—spirituality.

THE BOTTOM LINE

Where should a book on values end? Of all the important values of Christian experiences—values in the person, values in relationships, values in skills, competencies, abilities, family, possessions—we must decide what is important. Being human means making decisions and setting priorities. Being *fully* human means developing love.

Even if I might be eloquent in speaking and writing,
Even if I have special gifts from God,
including scientific understanding,
And benefit from vast libraries
and give evidence of great faith—
Without love all these are noisy, worthless, nothing.

The godly values of time and eternity will stand.
There are three basis values:
faith, hope, and love.
The greatest of these is love
(paraphrased from 1 Corinthians 13).

Glossary

ABSTRACT, as in *an abstract idea*. Concerned with theoretical and background matters; although a thing might be beautiful, beauty is abstract; if it's abstract, you can't touch it; contrast with *concrete*. Younger children don't handle abstract ideas very well.

ACTION, as in *moral action*. The doing of something; the act itself; behavior. An action may or may not be consistent with a person's moral values.

AESTHETIC, as in *aesthetic values*. Concerned with beauty, grace, elegance; taste in matters of art, music, and literature shows aesthetic values. Aesthetic values are not usually concerned with moral choices.

BEHAVIORISTIC, behaviorism, as in *behavioristic approaches* to teaching are manipulative. Usually contrasted with developmental or developmentalism. The Christian view of the responsibility and the integrity of the person is difficult to reconcile with behaviorism.

BELIEF, as in *religious belief*. What one holds to be true; a strongly held belief is a conviction. Belief is the ultimate ground for any deliberate choice.

CONCRETE, as in a *concrete idea*. Concerned with things or people that are "here and now"; anything "concrete" is solid enough to sit on, hold, or point at while you talk about it; contrast with *abstract*. Children are more likely to reason well about concrete experience.

CONSISTENT, as in *consistent response.* A response, reply, or action that is the same or very similar each time one reacts to the particular situation. A person who is consistent can be more effective as a moral example.

CONTENT, as in *the content of a moral judgment.* The matter of *what* is judged morally good or bad; e.g., "lying is wrong" is a content; contrast with *structure.* Content is the *what* of good and bad: what is right; what is wrong.

DEVELOPMENTAL, developmentalism, as in *developmental approaches to teaching* place a great deal of responsibility on the capabilities, decisions, and actions of the learner. Usually contrasted with *behavioristic* or *behaviorism.* The Christian view of the responsibility and the integrity of the person is consistent with developmentalism.

DISCIPLINE, as in *a discipline problem.* Behavior, especially in the sense of controlled, orderly behavior; also refers to the process of controlling behavior; one is either self-disciplined or can expect to be disciplined. Discipline is more than punishment. At its best, it means self-control.

ECOLOGY, ecological, as in *ecological view of human life.* Emphasizing the interrelatedness of all the functions and aspects of the human being. An ecological view of spiritual development sees it as related to all the aspects of a person's development.

EQUILIBRATION, as used by Piaget to refer to one important development process. Re-equilibration is the process of getting one's understanding "balanced out" again after encountering an idea or experience that doesn't fit into what one already believes. No one feels comfortable while off-balance.

ETHICAL, as in *an ethical problem.* Concerned with right and wrong; especially moral standards for human conduct. All ethical standards reflect moral values.

ETHICS, as in *a matter of ethics.* Concerned with the recognized and morally accepted standards of behavior. Ethics generally refers to statements or codes of moral standards.

EXTENDED FAMILY. A cultural variation of family style in which people of several generations live together as one unit, usually involving grandparents as well as children who are cousins. Americans generally tend not to think of "family" in terms of the extended family. In most of the societies of the world, the extended family is almost always consulted on important decisions.

FORMAL OPERATIONS. Refers to thought processes that are advanced; able to think abstract thoughts and to reason about complex matters. Thinking in terms of formal operations emerges in late childhood.

HOLISTIC (wholistic), as in *holistic view of human life*. Concerned with the whole rather than only with one part or with one part at a time. A holistic view of human life accepts a core of spiritual essence surrounded by a set of observable aspects of life, such as the physical reality, mental capability, emotional function, social interactions, and capability for moral judgments.

INCONSISTENCY. Unpredictable; makes observers uneasy because there is lack of pattern and logic in the behavior; contrast with *consistency*. Inconsistency of parents confuses children.

JUDGMENT, as in *moral judgment*. The mental processes by which a person decides whether or not a given act or value is good or bad, right or wrong. The judgment process has two parts: content and structure.

MORAL, as in *moral judgment*. Concerned with good and evil, not simply personal taste or preference; moral issues are, for a Christian, concerned with sin and righteousness. Humanists and Christians generally agree that when a decision or choice involves the welfare of one or more human beings, it involves *moral* judgments.

NUCLEAR FAMILY. Based on the idea of a center or nucleus, the nuclear family is one that centers around the mother and father; usually refers to the parents and children until their marriage. Nuclear family images are those most commonly associated with "family" in mass media and conversation in middle class United States and Canada.

OPERATIONS, as in *mental operations*. The processes of thinking: recalling, associating, reasoning, judging, etc.; used in reference to Piaget's conclusions to distinguish between concrete operations and formal operations, i.e., thinking about *things* versus thinking about *ideas*. Even as one talks about how a machine operates, it is possible to talk about how the mind operates.

PERCEPTION. The mental process in which things observed are converted into meanings—usually described as connecting the recall of previous experience with the thing being currently observed, e.g., a person *sees* an object moving across the scene, the mind *perceives* it to be a horse. Perceptions are apt to be quite individual and often unique.

QUEST, as in *quest for justice*. A search and effort to build upon what is being hunted; a quest is sometimes a lifetime commitment to seek out and to value, e.g., quest for truth. Faith, hope, and love are values toward which the Christian's life is a quest.

SELF-UNDERSTANDING. Becoming conscious of oneself in terms of positive and negative characteristics, strengths and weaknesses, tendencies and values; includes realistic appreciation and valuing of one's own worth. Self-understanding is essential for the Christian's spiritual development.

SENSORIMOTOR, as in *sensorimotor learning*. The use of muscles, activity, and the physical reaction systems is the basis for learning in infancy and early childhood. The child forms earliest impressions of the world by kicking against the crib slats, rubbing blankets, snuggling up to warm flesh, and putting things into the mouth; sensory: sense-oriented; motor: muscular movement. This learning by physical experience is what gets the mind into gear.

STRUCTURE, as in *the structure of a moral judgment*. The basis on which a content of moral judgment is held to be true and important; *why* one believes something is right or wrong. Simple statements about *what* is wrong or *what* is right are usually indications of one's moral *content*. On the other hand, "It's wrong *because* God says so" is more likely a matter of moral *structure*.

TASTE, as in *matters of taste and preference*. The simple preferences or choices in matters of custom (e.g., dress and hairstyle) or of aesthetics (e.g., what is good and beautiful in art and literature). Values are revealed in *taste* choices, but these are rarely concerned with moral matters.

VALUES, as in *moral values*. The choices, investments, and purposes which reflect a person's lifestyle and personal commitment; in moral matters, what a person holds to be right and wrong. *Values* covers a lot of ground, ranging from simple preferences in taste and aesthetics to important moral and spiritual matters.

Bibliography

Bronfenbrenner, Urie. *The Ecology of Human Development*. Cambridge: Harvard University Press, 1979.

Brown, George, Jr. Children's Faith. *Reformed Review* (Children and the Faith) 40, No. 3, Spring 1987.

Bryan, James. How Parents Teach Hypocrisy. *Psychology Today* 3, No. 7, 1969.

Cavalletti, Sofie. *The Religious Potential of the Child*. New York: Paulist Press, 1983.

Coles, Robert. *The Moral Life of Children*. Boston: Atlantic Monthly Press, 1986.

Dykstra, Craig. *Vision and Character: A Christian Educator's Alternative to Kohlberg*. New York: Paulist Press, 1981.

Elkind, David. *Children and Adolescents: Interpretive Essays on Jean Piaget*. New York: Oxford University Press, 1974.

Fowler, James. *Stages of Faith*. New York: Harper and Row, 1981.

Goldman, Ronald. *Readiness for Religion: A Basis for Developmental Religious Education*. New York: Seabury Press, 1965.

Gustafson, James. *Ethics from a Theocentric Perspective*. Chicago: University of Chicago Press, 1981.

Hartshorne, Hugh and Mark May. *Studies in the Nature of Character*. Studies in Deceit, No. 1. New York: Macmillan, 1928.

Hauerwas, Stanley. *A Community of Character*. Notre Dame: University of Notre Dame Press, 1981.

Keniston, Kenneth (and the Carnegie Council on Children). *All Our Children—the American Family Under Pressure*.

Kohlberg, Lawrence. The Development of Children's Orientations Toward a Moral Order. Part 1: Sequence in the Development of Moral Thought. *Vita Humana* 6:11-33, 1963.

——. Early Education: A Cognitive-Developmental View. *Child Development* 39 (December):1013-1062, 1968.

Kohlberg, Lawrence and Rochelle Mayer. Development as the Aim of Education. *Harvard Educational Review* 42, No. 4, 1972.

Kohlberg, Lawrence and Elliot Turiel. Moral Development and Moral Education. Edited by G. Lesser. *Psychology and Educational Practice*. Chicago: Scott, Foresman, 1971.

Lee, James Michael. Christian Religious Education and Moral Development. Edited by B. Munsey. *Moral Development, Moral Education, and Kohlberg*. Birmingham: Religious Education Press, 1980.

Maslow, Abraham H. *Motivation and Personality*. 2nd ed. New York: Harper and Row, 1970.

Moran, Gabriel. *Religious Education Development*. Minneapolis: Winston Press, 1983.

Ng, David and Virginia Thomas. *Children in the Worshiping Community*. Atlanta: John Knox Press, 1981.

Olthuis, James H. *I Pledge You My Troth: Marriage, Family, Friendship*. New York: Harper and Row, 1975.

Piaget, Jean. *The Origins of Intelligence in Children*. Translated by Margaret Cook. New York: International Universities Press, 1952.

Piaget, Jean and Barbel Inhelder. *Psychology of the Child*. New York: Basic Books, 1969.

Prior, Kenneth F.W. *The Gospel in a Pagan Society*. Downers Grove, Illinois: InterVarsity Press, 1975.

Sapp, Gary L., ed. *Handbook of Moral Development*. Birmingham: Religious Education Press, 1986.

Selman, Robert. The Relation of Role-taking to the Development of Moral Judgment in Children. *Child Development* 42:79-92, 1971.

Stone, Lawrence. *The Family, Sex, and Marriage in England 1500-1800*. New York: Harper and Row, 1977.

Stonehouse, Catherine M. *Patterns in Moral Development*. Dallas: Word, 1980.

Wolterstorff, Nicholas. *Educating for Responsible Action*. Grand Rapids: Eerdmans, 1980.

Woodward, Kenneth L., Mary Lord, Frank Maier, Donna M. Foote, and Phyllis Malamud. Saving the Family. *Newsweek*, 15 May, 1978.

Wren, Brian. *Education for Justice*. Maryknoll, New York: Orbis Books, 1977.

Wynne, Edward A. *Growing Up Suburban*. Austin: University of Texas Press, 1977.